people and their god

Jon Mayled

Nelson

Note to teachers

This book approaches the issues, beliefs and fundamental questions of life raised by the GCSE (Short Course) in Religious Education from the perspective of the sacred texts and teachings of Judaism, Christianity and Islam.

Frequently, students do not present their best work in examinations in this area because they find it easier to rely on sociological approaches to the questions asked rather than providing religious ones. It is hoped that this book will enable students to see these religious teachings in context and to appreciate that they are the basis for many of the strongly held beliefs which people have about the issues raised in Religious Education.

The book aims to cover the content of all the Short Course RE syllabuses from the perspective of these three religions. Within the confines of a limited number of pages it is never possible to say everything and to give every example and argument but it is designed to provide sufficient information for students and teachers to cover the course. The pictures have been chosen to stimulate discussion on broader aspects of the issues dealt with in each chapter. The Glossary aims to give simple definitions of the technical terms used in the text and, as far as possible, these are derived from the SCAA Glossary of Religious Terms published in June 1994.

NOTE: The phrase 'peace be upon him' is normally said by Muslims every time Prophet Muhammad's name is mentioned. For the sake of continuity, it has been omitted from the text. No disrespect to the Prophet (peace be upon him) is intended by this. Readers are requested to keep this in mind when reading.

Contents

Introduction

All through our lives we have to make decisions. These may be very simple such as 'which pair of trainers shall I wear today?' or 'what should I get my best friend as a birthday present?'

On the other hand, we often have to make more important decisions. These may affect the way in which we behave towards other people or the way in which we treat ourselves.

This book looks at how we make these decisions. Many people say that making decisions is a matter of common sense; that we decide what we want to do and do it. Very few of our decisions are this straightforward, however.

You are walking along a quiet street. On the pavement you spot a purse. There is no name or address inside the purse, but it contains £55. You have two main options. You do not decide to leave the purse where it is because you think the chances of the owner finding it are very small. Also, someone else may decide to pick it up. So, you can either keep the purse and the money and go out for a good time, or you can hand it in at the nearest police station.

Suppose that you do not think that there is much chance of the police being able to find the owner of the purse. You decide to keep the money for yourself. You did not steal the money, you were just fortunate enough to find it.

The following week you read an article in the local paper. A pensioner has been found dead in her flat from a heart attack. Neighbours say that she had been very depressed since she lost her purse containing £55 of her rent money.

You cannot improve the situation. You may feel sick and guilty about the fact that you could have prevented this old woman's suffering. If you still have the money, you may decide to give it to charity. It is still not your money to give away, but you might think that if you made an anonymous donation to an organisation such as Help the Aged, you would feel less guilty.

There are a number of issues here. First, there is how you make your decision about keeping the money or handing it in. Secondly, there is the question of why you now feel guilty and how you might deal with your guilt.

All these decisions are to do with our **conscience**.

Conscience is a sense of knowing that something is right or wrong. When babies are born, they survive on what we might refer to as a 'pleasure principle' (hedonism). They know, or at least they think they know, what they want: food, to be hugged, to be warm. They do not

The signs of the Zodiac.

consider how their demands affect other people. In fact, many of us do not take other people into account until we are much older and, perhaps, wiser. So somehow, we train our conscience, we learn to make decisions and to judge the effects of these on other people. Some people never learn to do this. If we are being totally honest, we can probably think of times when we have put ourselves first and ignored other people.

We might say that we learn these values from our families or our friends. This is true, but the real question is: where do these values and this sense of conscience come from in the first place? They are not simply floating around in the air, waiting for us to collect them as we grow older.

Questions like these have been asked ever since people have been able to think. There is no point in telling a dog or a cat that something is wrong. In the first place, despite what some owners claim, they will not understand what you are saying. Animals learn about what we regard as right and wrong by being punished or rewarded. If a dog comes when you call, then you may reward it with a pat or something to eat. If it eats your supper then it may be smacked. Animals will never learn that what they are doing is wrong *morally*, they just understand that if they do something which we do not like, they will be punished.

God and Adam, Michelangelo (1475–1564), the Sistine Chapel, Italy.

Babies are brought up in a similar way, by a process of reward and punishment. You may feel that school is not very different: if you keep the rules you may be rewarded, or at least not punished. The big difference between humans and other animals is that we can learn that things really are right or wrong. You may be hungry, but that does not give you the right to walk into a shop and steal something.

Rules and laws

In most cases, laws are laid down by the government. Every country has laws: you must drive on the left hand side of the road, you must go to school until you are sixteen, and so on.

Laws are designed to control a society and to make it a place where people can live together peacefully. We know that often this does not work, but a society without rules, an **anarchic** society, would probably be far worse to live in.

In addition to government laws, however, there are the rules which we try to live by which are designed to make the world a better place and to make us better people. These rules could be as follows:

You shall not murder.
You shall not steal.
You shall not commit adultery.
You shall not bear false witness (lie).
You shall not want someone else's possessions or belongings.

(Exodus 20: 13–17)

The first three of these are straightforward. You could argue that there are all sorts of circumstances where one or other of them may be broken, but that does not change the fact that they offer very basic standards for living within a society.

The final two are more complex. 'You shall not bear false witness' means that you should not lie about other people. The final statement is about greed. If we want something which belongs to somebody else, then we make ourselves unhappy and risk not getting on with other people because we are envious.

These statements come from the Ten Commandments. These Commandments or Laws are very old; they are part of the ancient history of the Jews, but every religion has a similar set of instructions.

These then, are religious rules. Many people say that religion is out of date. They may say that people need to live their lives in the real world and not worry about myths and legends which are thousands of years old. However, even if we agree with this, we cannot ignore the effect which religion continues to have on people's lives.

The role of religion

Religion is still the most important influence on the lives of most people in the world today. We may say that we do not believe in religion, and that it is nothing to do with us but it still affects many aspects of our lives.

All around us we find religious buildings reflecting the cultures and communities that live nearby. Holidays and school terms are often controlled by the timing of religious celebrations. Our lives are broken up into days and months, most of which are named after the gods of ancient religions.

Religion has been the cause of the majority of wars that have been fought in the world as people from different religious groups have sought to dominate one another. This does not mean that religion is a bad thing. Instead, it shows that many people do not tolerate each other when they encounter those who have different beliefs.

Religious belief has been with humanity since the very beginning. It is an attempt to explain those things for which we do not otherwise have an answer: why are we born? why do we suffer? what happens when we die? Also, as we have seen, it strongly influences what we call our conscience.

In this book we will be looking at the ways in which the three major religions of the Western world – Judaism, Christianity and Islam – continue to influence people's lives and their thinking.

1 *What is God?*

So, to start at the beginning:
>   Is there a thing we call 'God'?
>   If there is a God, what is it?
>   If God is a person is this person male or female?
>   And, anyway, how on earth can we hope to answer
>   these questions?

The simple answer is that we cannot answer any of these questions in any sort of 'scientific' manner. In order to do so, we would have to carry out an experiment again and again and reach the same result. Of course, we do not know what kind of experiment to carry out to answer these questions – so there are no results.

Most religious people see 'God' as a divine and supreme being who is totally good. They believe that God is so far beyond our experience and our thoughts that we cannot find any way to describe her or him. Despite this, Judaism, Christianity and Islam all represent God as male. Some followers of these religions, however, now say that this may leave out the aspects of God which we would normally think of as female. They claim that the only reason God is thought to be male is because it was men who founded these religions.

God has been described by religious traditions in different ways and there have been many different representations of God in art. Some religions, such as Hinduism, have attempted to draw and make statues of their Gods. They do not say that these images bear a resemblance to God, however. Instead, the images are made to help people to focus on a God who is otherwise too far beyond anything we can imagine. Islam and Judaism forbid their followers to try to draw or make images of God.

If we could truly describe God then we would have somehow limited him or her to something which is under our control. God becomes no more than human if we can describe him or her.

Try to think of the universe being infinite, that is, going on for ever. Then imagine travelling beyond every part of the universe that we can see with the strongest and most sophisticated scientific equipment. You soon reach a point which you cannot imagine any more. The idea is so vast that your brain begins to 'hurt' just trying to imagine it. Yet, if what religions say about God is true, then this being, or force, is infinitely larger and more difficult to think about than the entire universe which he or she created.

For centuries people have tried to answer questions about God and there are several arguments which have been put forward in an attempt to decide whether God exists or not:

Ontological
Anselm (1033-1109) said that because people described God as 'that than which nothing greater can be conceived', God must exist otherwise we could not produce this description.

Cosmological
Thomas Aquinas (1225-74) argued that something cannot come from nothing. Because there is a universe, someone or something must have brought it into existence. Aquinas said that this 'first cause' was God.

Design (Teleological)
William Paley (1734-1805) produced a theory which has become known as the Divine Watchmaker. If you found a watch in the street, you would assume that its parts had not come together by chance, but that someone had designed it. He then applied this argument to the world and so to God.

Experience
Some people have argued that, because people claim that miracles have happened and that they have had experience of God, God must exist.

Morality
How can we know the difference between right and wrong unless God has told us this?

All of these arguments have people who support or disagree with them, but they are still only arguments. None of them actually 'prove' that there is such a thing as God in a way which would be acceptable to a scientist.

Throughout the scriptures there are times when God appears to the Jews, but only in the Garden of Eden is there a suggestion of God in a human form:

> So God created man in his own image, in the image of God he created him; male and female he created them.
>
> (Genesis 1:27)

For the rest of the **Tenakh** (Jewish scriptures) God is sometimes a pillar of cloud or flame, and sometimes just a voice, as when he speaks to the prophet Elijah:

> Then a great and powerful wind tore the mountains apart and shattered the rocks before the Lord, but the Lord was not in the wind. After the wind there was an earthquake, but the Lord was not in the earthquake. After the earthquake came a fire, but the Lord was not in the fire. And after the fire came a gentle whisper.
>
> (1 Kings 19:11-12)

On other occasions God is shown as a powerful king:

> I saw the Lord seated on a throne, high and exalted, and the train of his robe filled the temple. Above him were seraphs, each with six wings: ... And they were calling to one another: 'Holy, holy, holy is the Lord Almighty; the whole earth is full of his glory.'
> At the sound of their voices the doorposts and thresholds shook and the temple was filled with smoke.
>
> (Isaiah 6:1-4)

Genesis, the first book of the Jewish scriptures, opens with a description of God as a Spirit creating the world:

> *In the beginning God created the heavens and the earth. Now the earth was formless and empty, darkness was over the surface of the deep, and the Spirit of God was hovering over the waters.*
>
> (Genesis 1:1-2)

Later, God speaks to Moses through a bush which is burning and Moses asks his name:

> *God said to Moses, 'I AM WHO I AM.'*
>
> (Exodus 3:14)

This is the first time that God gives himself a name but, of course, it is not very clear. In the Jewish scriptures, God's name is spelt with four consonants: YHWH (this is called the Tetragrammaton or 'four letters'). Jewish teaching says that the name is so holy that only the High Priest knew how to pronounce it. He only spoke it once a year, alone, in the Holy of Holies in the Temple at Jerusalem. When they see these four letters Jews usually say the name Adonai instead – this means Lord.

The Jewish scriptures say that Moses spoke to God:

> *As Moses went into the tent, the pillar of cloud would come down and stay at the entrance, while the Lord spoke with Moses… The Lord would speak to Moses face to face, as a man speaks with his friend.*
>
> (Exodus 33:9, 11)

Later, when Moses was receiving the Ten Commandments, he asked to see God:

> *And the Lord said, 'I will cause all my goodness to pass in front of you, and I will proclaim my name, the Lord, in your presence… But,' he said, 'you cannot see my face, for no-one may see me and live.' Then the Lord said, 'There is a place near me where you may stand on a rock. When my glory passes by, I will put you in a cleft in the rock and cover you with my hand until I have passed by. Then I will remove my hand and you will see my back; but my face must not be seen.'*
>
> (Exodus 33:19-23)

Jews believe that there is only one God and this is stated in one of the central Jewish prayers – the **Shema**. In the following version, the name of God is replaced by the Hebrew word 'Hashem':

> *Hear, O Israel: Hashem is our God, Hashem, the One and Only…*

Jews follow a way of life called **Halakhah** which means 'walking with God'. They live by all the 613 mitzvot (or rules) which are found in the five books of the Torah (Genesis, Exodus, Leviticus, Numbers and Deuteronomy). These books are believed to have been written by

Moses. Jews also follow the teachings in the Oral Torah, which God gave to Moses and were written down in the Talmud.

Moses and the Burning Bush, *William Blake (1757–1828)*

Persecution of the Jews

Despite all their attempts to live according to the will of God, Jews have been persecuted throughout history and have suffered for their religion. Their belief in God, however, is still strong.

There are many stories of Jews being defeated in battles, being taken into slavery and being killed, simply because they were Jews. The majority of the Jews were driven out of Israel in the first century CE and it did not become their own country again until 1948. During those 900 years Jews lived all over the world, at first accepted by people and later persecuted by them.

The most recent disaster to hit the Jews was the **Shoah** or **Holocaust** of the Second World War. The Chancellor of Germany, Adolf Hitler, told his people that he was going to create a 'Master Race'. This would consist of Aryan people, that is, tall with blonde hair and blue eyes. At that time, many German Jews were in powerful financial positions. Hitler said that they were the main cause of all Germany's problems and that they must be stopped.

In an event called the Final Solution, he attempted to have all the Jews in Europe collected together in camps in Germany and Poland, such as Auschwitz-Birkenau, Sobibór and Treblinka. Here they were gassed. Six million Jews and other 'undesirables' such as gypsies, Communists, Slavs and homosexuals, were murdered by order of the German government.

Hitler was not, of course, successful and after his defeat, Judaism began to grow once more. It would not be surprising, however, if some Jews felt that their God had let them down. Many Jews did say that 'God died in Auschwitz' or that 'God was not in Auschwitz' but for others the tragedy served only to strengthen their faith. Some decided that perhaps their earlier faith was too simple and that the events of the Holocaust required them to rethink how they lived. Nevertheless their belief in God continues.

This is a medieval drawing which tries to show the Trinity. In the three corner circles are the words (in Latin) Pater – Father, Filius – Son and Sanctus Spiritus – Holy Spirit. In the centre is Deus – God. The words around the outside show that the Father non est (is not) the Son, the Son is not the Spirit, etc. The other lines show that the Father est (is) God, the Son is God and the Spirit is God.

The **Trinity** is central to Christian belief and is a teaching which makes Christianity different from all other religions. The Trinity is the three 'persons' or 'natures' of God. The Creed of St Athanasius said:

So the Father is God, the Son is God : and the Holy Spirit is God.
So likewise the Father is Lord, the Son Lord : and the Holy Spirit Lord.
And yet not three Lords : but one Lord.

Other statements about the Trinity are found in the Nicene Creed:

We believe in one God, the Father, the almighty, maker of heaven and earth…
We believe in one Lord, Jesus Christ, the only Son of God, eternally begotten of the Father, true God from true God, begotten not made, of one Being with the Father…
We believe in the Holy Spirit, the Lord, the giver of life, who proceeds from the Father and the Son. With the Father and the Son he is worshipped and glorified. He has spoken through the Prophets.

Many people have tried to represent the Trinity to show the relationship among these three 'Persons': God the Father, God the Son and God the Holy Spirit. Some people have said that the Trinity can be represented by water. It can be a fluid, it can be frozen and become solid, or it can be heated when it becomes steam, but all the time it is still water (H_2O).

The Ancient of Days, *William Blake (1757–1828)*

Christians believe that the God of the Jews, and the God of the Old and New Testament is one God.

- This God is sometimes described as God the Father, the Creator of all life, this is the God to whom Jesus was praying in the Lord's Prayer.
- Sometimes he is God the Son, Jesus Christ, who chose to take on the form of a human being and to teach people God's will. Jesus of Nazareth, the Messiah of Christianity, is important because although he was innocent he willingly died on the cross to save people from their sins. When Jesus rose from the dead three days after he was killed, he showed that death was not the end and that God had power over death. Because of this, people have a chance to go to heaven when they die.
- Sometimes he is God the Holy Spirit who inspires people and gives them strength.

The God who appears in the Old Testament seems different from the God whom Jesus speaks of as 'Father'. However, Christians believe that the whole Bible is the revealed Word of God and that these differences show the changing relationship between God and humanity over thousands of years.

All Scripture is God-breathed and is useful for teaching, rebuking, correcting and training in righteousness, so that the man of God may be thoroughly equipped for every good work.

(2 Timothy 3:16–17)

In the Bible God and God's teachings are revealed through the Prophets such as Isaiah, Jeremiah and John the Baptist. In the Old Testament there are references to a Messiah who will come from God to lead the people:

For to us a child is born, to us a son is given, and the government will be on his shoulders. And he will be called Wonderful Counsellor, Mighty God, Everlasting Father, Prince of Peace. Of the increase of his government and peace there will be no end. He will reign on David's throne and over his kingdom, establishing and upholding it with justice and righteousness from that time on and for ever.

(Isaiah 9:6–7)

In the New Testament, Jesus is seen as this Messiah, the Son of God:

Today in the town of David a Saviour has been born to you; he is Christ the Lord.

(Luke 2:11)

Christians describe God in many different ways: as a judge and ruler, as a father, as a great and mysterious power, as a friend and saviour and, particularly, as love. All these are aspects of the Christian God. Rather than showing that this God is inconsistent, however, they indicate that God is so much beyond humanity's understanding that it is impossible for people to know how to describe him.

The Lord's Prayer
Our Father in heaven,
hallowed be your name,
your kingdom come,
your will be done,
on earth as it is in heaven.
Give us today our daily bread.
Forgive us our sins as we forgive those who sin against us.
Lead us not into temptation but deliver us from evil.

Here is a trustworthy saying that deserves full acceptance: Christ Jesus came into the world to save sinners—of whom I am the worst. But for that very reason I was shown mercy so that in me, the worst of sinners, Christ Jesus might display his unlimited patience as an example for those who would believe on him and receive eternal life. Now to the King eternal, immortal, invisible, the only God, be honour and glory for ever and ever. Amen.

(1 Timothy 1:15–17)

Christ in Glory, *Hubert and Jan van Eyck*

The great importance of Allah is stressed in **salah**, daily prayers. The **adhan**, or call to prayer, has the following statements:

> *Allah is the Greatest*
> *Allah is the Greatest*
> *Allah is the Greatest*
> *Allah is the Greatest*
> *I bear witness that there is no god but Allah*
> *I bear witness that there is no god but Allah*
> *I bear witness that Muhammad is Allah's messenger*
> *I bear witness that Muhammad is Allah's messenger*
> *Rush to prayer*
> *Rush to prayer*
> *Rush to success*
> *Rush to success*
> *Allah is the Greatest*
> *Allah is the Greatest*
> *There is no god but Allah*

Among the 99 names of Allah are:

> *the One and Only, the Living One, the Subsisting, the Real Truth, the Sublime, the Wise, the Omnipotent, the Hearer, the Seer, the Omniscient, the Witness, the Protector, the Benefactor, the Merciful, and the Constant Forgiver.*

Tradition says that the hundredth name is a secret, known only to camels. Prophet Muhammad taught that:

> There are ninety-nine names that are Allah's alone. Whoever, learns, understands and enumerates them enters Paradise and achieves eternal salvation.

Allah (God) is central to a Muslim's life and beliefs. A statement of the seven basic beliefs of Islam is contained in Al-Imanul Mufassal:

> *I believe in Allah, in His angels, in His books, in His messengers, in the Last Day and in the fact that everything good or bad is decided by Allah, the Almighty, and in the Life after Death.*

The **Shahadah**, the statement which forms the first Pillar of Islam, states the importance of Allah:

> *La ilaha illal lahu muhammadur rasulul lah*
> *There is no god but Allah, Muhammad is the messenger of Allah*

Tawhid – the 'oneness' of Allah – is clearly expressed in the Qur'an and is the most important aspect of Islamic belief:

> *Say: He is God, the One and Only; God, the Eternal, Absolute; He begetteth not, nor is He begotten; And there is none like unto Him.*
>
> (Surah 112:1–4)

Muslims say that they must let Tawhid grow in their hearts and let it shape and control the whole of their lives. By following Tawhid, a Muslim becomes contented, trusting in God and dedicates their life to seeking God's pleasure.

Al-Qadr is a belief that Allah has laid down a pre-determined course for the world and knows the destiny of every living creature. However, this does not mean that people do not have free will. Allah made humans his Khalifahs, or agents, on earth. People are not forced to obey Allah's will and may choose to disobey him, but he knows what decisions people will make. Humans are judged on these decisions at **Akhirah**, the Day of Judgement.

Allah communicates with humanity by **Risalah** – the Prophets. According to the Prophet Muhammad there are 124,000 Prophets, but only 25 are mentioned in the Qur'an. Many of these Prophets are the same people that are found in the Jewish and Christian scriptures, showing part of the common origins of these three 'Religions of the Book'.

The Qur'an is the holy book of Islam but other books are mentioned in it as being revealed by God:

Zabur	Psalms of David
Tawrat	Torah of Moses
Injil	Gospels of the New Testament
Suhuf-i-Ibrahim	Scrolls of Abraham

Islam says that only the Qur'an still exists in its original form and that these other revealed books have been changed from the true words of God.

The Qur'an was revealed to the Prophet Muhammad by the Angel Jibril over a period of 23 years. Because Muhammad could not read or write, he memorised the Qur'an as he heard it and then dictated it to his secretary Zaid Bin Thabit. It was not compiled as one book until after his death. Since then it has remained unchanged and Muslims say that it cannot be translated into any other language because that would change the word of Allah.

The first revelation of the Qur'an stresses the importance of the message of God and the fact that the Prophet Muhammad was to repeat them:

Proclaim! In the name of thy Lord and Cherisher, Who created – created man, out of a (mere) clot of congealed blood: Proclaim! And thy Lord Is Most Bountiful,–He who taught (the use of) the pen, – taught man that which he knew not.

(Surah 96:1–5)

The final revelation was made shortly before the Prophet's death:

This day have I perfected your religion for you, completed My favour upon you, And have chosen for you Islam as your religion.

(Surah 5:4)

PROPHETS OF ISLAM

Quranic name	Biblical name
Adam	Adam
Idris	Enoch
Nuh	Noah
Hud	
Salih	Salih
Ibrahim	Abraham
Isma'il	Ishmael
Ishaq	Isaac
Lut	Lot
Ya'qub	Jacob
Yusuf	Joseph
Shu'aib	
Ayyub	Job
Musa	Moses
Harun	Aaron
Dhu'l-kifl	Ezekiel
Dawud	David
Sulamain	Solomon
Ilias	Elias
Al-Yasa'	Elisha
Yunus	Jonah
Zakariyya	Zechariah
Yahya	John
'Isa	Jesus
Muhammad	

Muhammad was the last Prophet and received the final revelation from God. He is sometimes called the 'Seal of the Prophets'.

The Shahadah in Islamic calligraphy.

Summary

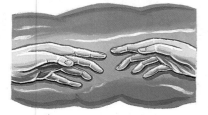

Perhaps, at the end of this chapter, you are no clearer than you were before about 'What God is', but you have now seen some of the arguments which people use to 'prove' that there is, or is not, a God and how different religions see their God.

This chapter is particularly important because without some sort of belief in God, there would probably be no religion. What is certain is that until someone can prove that God does, or does not, exist then God will be a matter of faith and belief for religious people and the arguments will continue.

God dividing the Waters and Earth, *Michelangelo (1475–1564)*

1 What do you understand by:

revelation

the ontological, cosmological and teleological arguments

arguments from experience and morality

scientific proof

infinity and eternity

analogy, metaphor and symbolism?

2 Look at the arguments *for* the existence of God. Which do you think are the most convincing and unconvincing arguments? Why?

3 Make a list of some of the different ways in which God is described and explain why these descriptions are used.

4 Choose one religion and try to write a description of God. You may decide to try to write a physical description, to use symbolic language or to describe the characteristics of God.

5 Explain why some religious people may say that they 'know' God exists.

6 How much do you think it would matter if people discovered that God was actually female?

2 How can we 'know'?

It is sometimes very difficult to know what we mean by 'truth'. The truth is usually something which is definitely known to be a fact. People say 'I want the truth' or 'I want to get to the truth', and this suggests that when they hear or find the truth they will recognise it. On the other hand, some people say that for something to be true, we must have evidence which proves that truth.

Religions, however, do not have any evidence for their beliefs which we can test scientifically. People cannot say things like 'whenever I'm short of money I pray to God and he or she gives me some'. Even if they did, we would probably not believe them; at the most we would say that it was a coincidence, because this is not how experience suggests God works.

There are various types of truth which we might consider:

- **Scientific truth** is perhaps the easiest sort of truth to understand. When a scientist conducts an experiment which can be repeated over and over again with the same results, this establishes a truth – for example, the way in which two chemicals will react if they are mixed together. This truth is sometimes called 'empirical truth'.
- **Historical truth** is when evidence of something proves that a particular event took place in the past.
- **Moral truth** is a suggestion that we might 'know' what is right or wrong without necessarily being able to prove it.
- **Aesthetic** or **artistic truth** can be found in novels, pictures, films and even, perhaps, music. It is the idea that, for example, although what we are reading or watching may be a work of fiction which a person created, the way in which people behave is 'true to human nature'.
- **Spiritual truth** is the type of truth which we find in religion. This is the idea that people believe in a religion and follow it in order to discover what the 'real truth' is, the truth which comes from God.

Religious people often say that there is an 'absolute truth' because they believe in the teachings of their religion. People who belong to one religion and accept its claims to truth, may feel that all other religions are wrong and do not have *the* truth.

In this chapter we will look at what religions claim to be their truth and why.

Richard Nixon (1913–94). President of the USA 1972–74, forced to resign because of the Watergate scandal.

A scientific experiment

Moses bringing the Ten Commandments to the Jews.

For Jews the truth lies in their holy scriptures, the Torah, and in their special relationship with God.

The centre of Jewish belief is contained in the prayer called the Shema:

Hear, O Israel: The Lord our God, the Lord is one. Love the Lord your God with all your heart and with all your soul and with all your strength. These commandments that I give you today are to be upon your hearts. Impress them on your children. Talk about them when you sit at home and when you walk along the road, when you lie down and when you get up. Tie them as symbols on your hands and bind them on your foreheads. Write them on the door-frames of your houses and on your gates.

(Deuteronomy 6:4-9)

This statement of belief in one God is at the centre of Jewish life.

Judaism teaches that Abraham entered into a special relationship with God called a **covenant**. This was an agreement between them that Abraham and his family would worship one God and no others, and that God would look after his family and descendants for ever.

I will surely bless you and make your descendants as numerous as the stars in the sky and as the sand on the seashore. Your descendants will take possession of the cities of their enemies, and through your offspring all nations on earth will be blessed, because you have obeyed me.

(Genesis 22:17-18)

This covenant relationship is broken again and again by the Jews in the Bible, but God always forgives them when they repent and so the relationship continues.

The Torah is of great importance to Jews. It contains five books which, in English, are called Genesis, Exodus, Leviticus, Numbers and Deuteronomy. Jewish tradition teaches that these five books were all written by Moses after they were revealed to him by God. Jews do not always claim that every word in the Torah is literally true and some believe that it may be allegorical. For example, the story of Creation and of Adam and Eve may not be historical fact, but it does contain essential truths about God and about human nature.

If it is accepted that these books were all written by Moses, there are still some difficult questions to answer. It may be possible that God told Moses about the creation of the world and the events which took place before he was born. However, many Progressive Jews have found it difficult to accept some things, such as Moses writing the account of his own death at the end of Deuteronomy.

The Torah is treated with great respect by all Jews. It is handwritten by a scribe on large pages made of animal skin and is placed on long rollers. These scrolls are decorated with covers and hung with bells and other decorations. When they are not in use the scrolls are kept in a cupboard in the synagogue called the **Aron Hakodesh** (the ark). When they are being read they are not touched by hand but a **yad** (pointer) is used so that the reader can follow the text.

Orthodox Jews believe that the Torah must be accepted as the Word of God and, therefore, the teachings cannot be altered. Progressive Jews, however, argue that it must be interpreted to suit the times in which it is being read.

There are places in the Torah where the text is sometimes unclear and difficult to understand, but tradition has provided an explanation of these. Where there are difficulties in interpreting the text, the Talmud or Oral Torah is used. Jews believe that God gave Moses the Oral Torah at the same time as the Written Torah and that it is intended to be used to interpret the written text.

The Talmud is a collection of the teachings of many generations of Rabbis arguing and discussing the texts of the Torah and offering explanations as to the exact meaning of them. This tradition of scholarly discussion is a very important part of Jewish teaching about the Torah. It does not go as far as Biblical Criticism, however, and Orthodox Jews do not look at the text to ask how it was written, or who wrote it and when. For them, these questions are answered by the belief that it was all written by Moses. On the rare occasions when a piece of text is unintelligible but can be understood if one word is altered, a rule called **keri** – read, and **k'tiv** – written is used and the 'correct' word is read in place of the one which is actually written.

The respect given to the Torah and the mitzvot (laws) which it contains, shows its great importance to Jews as a document which contains the truth about God and about their relationship with him.

Another kind of truth is the way in which Jewish life is seen as a reflection of belief in God. The way Jews dress, eat, celebrate festivals, keep the Sabbath and pray are all aspects of this belief.

The Torah contains the Ten Commandments (Exodus 20:1-17), but these are only ten of the 613 mitzvot which Jews live by. By living these out in their daily lives, Jews demonstrate their belief in God and the covenant relationship. They also live in preparation for the coming of the Messiah which is promised in the Bible.

A student reading the Torah, using a yad.

The Nicene Creed

We believe in one God,
the Father, the Almighty,
maker of heaven and earth,
of all that is, seen and unseen.

We believe in one Lord, Jesus Christ,
the only Son of God,
eternally begotten of the Father,
God from God, Light from Light,
true God from true God,
begotten, not made,
of one Being with the Father.
Through him all things were made.
For us men and for our salvation
he came down from heaven:
by the power of the Holy Spirit
he became incarnate from the
Virgin Mary, and was made man.

For our sake he was crucified
under Pontius Pilate;
he suffered death and was buried.
On the third day he rose again
in accordance with the
Scriptures;
he ascended into heaven
and is seated at the right hand
of the Father.
He will come again in glory to
judge the living and the dead,
and his kingdom will have no
end.

We believe in the Holy Spirit,
the Lord, the giver of life,
who proceeds from the Father
and the Son.
With the Father and the Son he
is worshipped and glorified.
He has spoken through the
Prophets.
We believe in one holy catholic
and apostolic Church.
We acknowledge one baptism
for the forgiveness of sins.
We look for the resurrection of
the dead,
and the life of the world to
come.

For Christians, the truth lies in belief in Jesus Christ who said:

I am the way and the truth and the life.

(John 14:6).

Christian belief is stated in the Creeds. Christians also have a very strong belief in the Bible as being the revealed Word of God. The Bible is seen as different from any other book because it contains God's word and, therefore, is believed to be true.

Christians have different views about the Bible:

- **Inerrancy** – this is a belief that every word of the Bible is absolutely true and that it is free from any kind of error or mistake.
- **Typology** – this view sees the stories in the Bible as symbolic. The truth is represented in stories but the stories themselves may not be true.
- **Allegory** – it has been suggested by some people that it is possible to read the Bible literally as well as to see it as a series of stories which contain the truth about God.

Many Christians say that the Bible is very old and needs to be interpreted for today. They may look to the clergy or theologians to explain what the Bible 'really' says about how they should live. Some Christians, however, believe that this means placing human beings in a higher position of authority than the Bible itself.

Christians disagree about this. Some will say that the Bible is, indeed, completely free from any mistakes or errors at all. When they find something in the Bible which they cannot understand, or where one verse seems to disagree with another one, they will say that this is simply because it is the Word of God; they are not intelligent enough, or good enough Christians to understand it. These sorts of problems arise when people look at the account of Jesus' last days in Jerusalem in the four Gospels and it appears that the dates and events are different.

Other Christians believe that, although the Bible is the Word of God, it was written down by human beings and so, naturally, it may contain mistakes and errors. They are not saying that the Bible is, therefore, any less important. They believe that people should read it carefully in order to understand what it is saying rather than attempting to take every word literally. They also point out that the version of the Bible which most people read is a translation from several ancient languages such as Hebrew, Aramaic and Greek. Scholars are still uncertain about the original meaning of some of the words. In addition, the Hebrew Bible has no punctuation or vowels, so it is possible that there may be some sections which are not translated in a way which exactly explains the original meaning.

In the last two hundred years, scholars have read the Bible very closely. Many have said that they can see evidence of the writing of different people working at different times. This has upset some Christians who take the text of the Bible very literally. Others say that this does not matter, if these people were inspired by God then the teachings of the Bible are still true.

For Christians, therefore, the Bible has moral truth and spiritual truth. It is possible that some of its stories, even though they may not be literally true, still have aesthetic truth. It has always been very difficult to prove historically that the things written down in the Bible actually happened.

Another very important part of the truth, for Christians, is the way in which they lead their lives. A life of a Christian, and in particular the way in which they treat other people, is an expression of their belief in God and in Jesus. By following the teachings of Jesus written in the New Testament, Christians are living according to God's will and so they are showing their belief in him.

The Christian Bible has been translated into more than one hundred languages.

Jimmy Lee Swaggart (1935–), an American evangelist caught up in incidents which indicated his involvement with prostitutes.

His Holiness Pope John Paul II.

At the centre of Muslim belief is the Shahadah and the Qur'an.

The Shahadah is the first Pillar of Islam and the central statement of belief:

There is no god but Allah, Muhammad is the messenger of Allah.

The Qur'an is the sacred book of Islam and, in some ways, is very different from the books of Judaism and Christianity.

Muslims say that the Qur'an was revealed to Prophet Muhammad by the angel Jibril and contains the actual words of Allah.

In 611 CE, Muhammad, then aged forty, was meditating in a cave. Jibril appeared to him and ordered him to read, but Muhammad said that he could not read. This happened three times and eventually the angel said:

Proclaim! In the name of thy Lord and Cherisher, who created – created man, out of a (mere) clot of congealed blood: Proclaim! And thy Lord Is Most Bountiful,–he who taught (the use of) the pen, – taught man that which he knew not.

(Surah 96:1–5)

Muhammad recited these words and then the angel said, 'O Muhammad, you are the messenger of Allah and I am Jibril', and left. Muhammad continued to receive visits from Jibril over the next 23 years. Finally, just before his death, he received the final verse:

This day have I perfected your religion for you, completed My favour upon you, and have chosen for you Islam as your religion.

(Surah 5:4)

Pages from the Holy Qur'an.

Prophet Muhammad remained illiterate throughout his life, so the Qur'an was written down by his followers from his recitation. Every copy of the Qur'an records these words of Allah, completely unchanged from the manner in which they were received by Muhammad. For this reason, versions of the Qur'an in languages other than Arabic, are not called 'translations' because Muslims say that it is not possible to translate successfully God's words into any other language.

The Qur'an is not written in chronological order. Surah 1 is the shortest and is then followed by the longest Surah and they grow shorter to the last which is 114.

No form of critical study of the Qur'an is undertaken because it is the Word of Allah. Every word is seen as a direct revelation, so there is no idea of discussing who wrote it and why. Islam does not consider these ideas as they would be irrelevant and disrespectful.

The Qur'an is seen as unchanging, unchangeable and untranslatable **Iman** (faith), and is regarded as the complete and final book of guidance from Allah for the whole of humanity for ever.

In this way the Qur'an and the teachings of Islam are regarded as absolute truth. It can be said that Muslims do not, therefore, have to believe because they actually know these teachings to be true.

Muslim life is an expression of Islam (submission) to the will of Allah and is lived according to the words of the Qur'an and following the teaching and example of Prophet Muhammad. These principles can all be found in the last sermon which Muhammad preached on Mount Arafat at the end of the Hajj.

Muhammad's sermon on Mount Arafat at the end of Hajj.

'O people, listen to my words carefully, for I know not whether I would meet you again on such an occasion. O people, just as you regard this month, this day, this city as sacred, so regard the lip and property of every Muslim as a sacred trust. Remember that you will indeed appear before Allah and answer for your actions.

Return the things kept with you as a trust to their rightful owners. All dues of interest shall stand cancelled and you will have only your capital back; Allah has forbidden interest, and I cancel the dues of interest payable to my uncle 'Abbas bin 'Abdul Muttalib....O people, none is higher than the other unless he is higher in obedience to Allah. No Arab is superior to a non-Arab except in piety.

O people, reflect on my words. I leave behind me two things, the Qur'an and my example, and if you follow these, you will not fail.

Listen to me carefully! Worship Allah and offer Salah, observe Saum in the month of Ramadan and pay Zakah.

O people, be mindful of those who work under you. Feed and clothe them as you feed and clothe yourselves.

O people, no prophet or messenger will come after me and no new faith will emerge. All those who listen to me shall pass on my words to others, and those to others again.'

(Hadith)

Ayatollah Khomeini (1900–89) religious and political leader of Iran.

Summary

The answer to the questions about religious truth appears to be that each of these religions regards its scriptures and the teachings within them to be true because they were revealed by God. We are not concerned about which one of them is actually true – that is something which people will never agree on.

Each religion, therefore, finds truth in the revealed Word of God in its scriptures, as well as the truth which they demonstrate in how they live their daily lives.

1 What do you understand by:

truth

proof

evidence

belief

revelation

authority?

2 Consider whether it matters that we cannot test religions in the way we test scientific truth.

3 Do you think it is possible for religious teachings to be true even if there are no historical facts to support them?

4 How far would you agree with the idea that scriptures need bringing up to date?

5 Does it matter if followers of a religion have different ideas about whether the scriptures are true or not?

6 Do you think that the statements of belief are more important for religions than their scriptures?

7 How far might it affect believers of one of these religions if someone proved that their scriptures were simply 'made up' by an ordinary person? Would it mean that their religion was no longer 'true'?

3 The case of Science v. Religion

Many religious traditions have a belief that God created the world and, in their sacred writings, have a description of God's act of Creation. No one can be sure about where these creation stories come from, or whether any of them are true or not. From what these stories say, however, we can be fairly sure that there was no human being there to witness what happened.

In their Creation stories, religions have sought to explain how God created the earth and all forms of life, from plants and insects to human beings. In most cases, these descriptions show God making the world, the earth, the sky, the seas, and then creating plant life, animals and finally, humans.

Cosmology is the science which deals with the origin and structure of the universe. It does not accept the idea that God created the earth, the other planets, the sun, moon and stars in the way it is told in creation stories. Instead, it has produced theories of how the universe began based on scientific evidence, such as the Big Bang theory. The science of cosmology appears to challenge religious views of Creation.

Charles Darwin and his theories became popular subjects for cartoonists.

Evolution is the theory that higher forms of life have gradually arisen from lower forms. Like cosmology, the theory is also based on scientific evidence and discovery. It was made famous by the publication, in 1859, of *On the Origin of Species* by Charles Darwin. He produced his theory by looking at fossils and at the many different varieties of animal life. His theory suggests that life on earth began with a very simple single cell and that life forms gradually evolved and developed from this cell. We see this development in the huge variety of plant and animal life found on the earth.

Many religious people have challenged both scientific views saying that they are untrue because they are at variance with the Creation stories. When Darwin's book was first published, Philip Gosse, an eminent geologist, claimed that Darwin was wrong in his theories. He said that the fossils which were found in rocks were simply placed there by God in order to test the faith of Christians.

Different religious traditions also claim that God can perform miracles which seem to defy the laws of science. Scientists say it is difficult to understand why God should want to break the laws which he created, simply to strengthen people's beliefs. In the same way, we might ask why miracles apparently happened regularly in the past, but rarely occur today when so many people are still starving and suffering from disasters.

The account of Creation in the Jewish scriptures is found in the book of Genesis, the first book of the Torah. The Torah is sometimes called the Five Books of Moses: Genesis, Exodus, Leviticus, Numbers and Deuteronomy.

The mushroom cloud formed by the explosion of a nuclear bomb.

The Jewish belief is that these books were written down by Moses, but were revealed to him by God. They are considered to be the 'Word of God', and true accounts of events.

One of the difficulties with accepting that they are all true is that in some places, there are two or more accounts of an event and the versions appear to disagree with one another. Some Jews say that this is because we do not understand them properly, and they would then offer an explanation. Progressive Jews, on the other hand, say that the reason for these differences is that the accounts were written by different people at different times and only later put together in the Torah. Progressive Jews do not say that the Torah is not the Word of God, but they accept that it was written down by more than one human being and not simply revealed to Moses.

An example of how the accounts in the Torah can differ is evident in the story of the creation of human beings. In the first chapter of Genesis it says:

So God created man in his own image, in the image of God he created him; male and female he created them.

(Genesis 1:27)

while the version in chapter two is:

the LORD God formed the man from the dust of the ground and breathed into his nostrils the breath of life, and the man became a living being. So the LORD God caused the man to fall into a deep sleep; and while he was sleeping, he took one of the man's ribs and closed up the place with flesh. Then the LORD God made a woman from the rib he had taken out of the man, and he brought her to the man. The man said, 'This is now bone of my bones and flesh of my flesh; she shall be called "woman", for she was taken out of man.'

(Genesis 2:7, 21–23)

Some people have said that these are two versions of the same event. Others say that it shows that there are two different groups of people writing who have different attitudes towards the relationship between men and women. The first account (which some scholars believe was written much later than the second one) shows God creating man and woman at the same time and so they appear equal. In the second account, it appears that man is created first and woman exists only as part of him. This version has led some people to argue that God intended women to be under the authority of men and that men are more important in God's eyes.

Cosmology and evolution

A belief that the Torah is all the work of Moses has caused difficulties for some Jews in accepting modern scientific explanations of Creation and evolution. Many Jews today, however, see the book of Genesis as an attempt to understand the existence of life and an explanation of the work of God as Creator, Sustainer and Provider to his Creation.

Miracles

There are many stories of miracles in the Torah, in particular, the accounts of Moses and his stick which turned into a snake; the plagues of Egypt; the parting of the Red Sea; and the food which the Israelites were given by God in the desert. To believe in these as actual facts means accepting that God will intervene and break physical laws in order to help his people. While there is no reason why an omnipotent God cannot do this, many people believe that it seems unlikely that God would create something as complex as the universe, and then decide to break its rules. Again, people have offered simpler explanations for these events.

> *Then Moses stretched out his hand over the sea, and all that night the Lord drove the sea back with a strong east wind and turned it into dry land. The waters were divided, and the Israelites went through the sea on dry ground, with a wall of water on their right and on their left.*
>
> (Exodus 14:21-22)

This account of the crossing of the Red Sea suggests that it was a strong wind which parted the waters, and some people have said that this might have happened naturally.

For many Jews, it does not matter whether these miracles are true, or an attempt to understand God. They believe that God was teaching his people and looking after them.

The view of God as Creator, Sustainer and Provider looking after the world is expressed in the Book of Psalms in the Jewish scriptures:

O Lord, our Lord, how majestic is your name in all the earth!
You have set your glory above the heavens.
From the lips of children and infants you have ordained praise because of your enemies, to silence the foe and the avenger.
When I consider your heavens, the work of your fingers, the moon and the stars, which you have set in place, what is man that you are mindful of him, the son of man that you care for him?
You made him a little lower than the heavenly beings and crowned him with glory and honour.
You made him ruler over the works of your hands; you put everything under his feet: all flocks and herds, and the beasts of the field, the birds of the air, and the fish of the sea, all that swim the paths of the seas.
O Lord, our Lord, how majestic is your name in all the earth!

(Psalm 8)

Although some Christians have had difficulty in accepting theories of cosmology, they have found more problems accepting the theory of evolution.

The biblical account of Creation shows that God created the world in a particular order:

Day One:	heaven and earth, light and dark
Day Two:	separation of the earth and the sky
Day Three:	seas and land, plants and trees
Day Four:	sun, moon and stars
Day Five:	fish and birds
Day Six:	animals and people

According to the Christian Bible, God created the world and all forms of life:

In the beginning God created the heavens and the earth. Now the earth was formless and empty, darkness was over the surface of the deep, and the Spirit of God was hovering over the waters.

(Genesis 1: 1–2)

Some Christians believe that this account of Creation should be taken literally and, therefore, God did create the world in a period of six days. In the seventeenth century, an English Bishop James Ussher, tried to work out the exact time of the creation of the world and calculated that it was at 9am on October 26 4004 BCE.

Today, many people would laugh at this attempt to work out a scientific issue by using the Bible as though it was a totally accurate scientific account. Nevertheless, it is not necessary to dismiss biblical accounts of Creation simply because we can now use modern scientific methods to discover what happened during the creation of the world.

Many Christians would now say that the Bible and science answer two different questions:

Science answers the question of *how* the world was created while religion explains *why*.

They may also argue that the circumstances for the production of life in the universe are so exact that it seems impossible that they could have simply come about by chance. God is necessary as a 'prime mover' for Creation to have taken place.

An alchemist at work in a laboratory. From an illustration dated 1508.

Cosmology and evolution

Many people would now accept the 'Big Bang' theory of the creation of the universe: that at the beginning of time, there was an enormous explosion. The universe we now see is the result of the explosion, and its effects are still going on today as the galaxies continue to move away from each other.

If this theory is correct, it would mean that God must have been present before the Big Bang took place. In the fourth century, St Augustine argued that, as time was a part of the world, God must have invented time at the same point as the rest of Creation.

Scientific evidence proves that life forms evolved over millions of years, so, today, it would be hard for anyone to argue that the world could have been created in six days. It was not until 1996, however, that the

Roman Catholic Church officially accepted that scientific theories of evolution were correct.

As early as the fourth century, St Augustine had anticipated this when he said: 'In the beginning were created only germs or causes of the forms of life which were afterwards to be developed in gradual course'.

His ideas about Creation are very similar to the theory of a gradual evolution. The biblical account is not wrong, therefore, as it does show the process of gradual evolution. It is simply that it is not to be interpreted literally.

The account of Creation in Genesis is designed to explain the relationship between God and nature. Like many of the accounts of Creation in other religions, it explains the relationship without entering into a scientific debate. Nevertheless, some fundamentalist Christians have found it impossible to accept that humans evolved and are related to apes, even though scientific research proves that this is so.

Miracles

Many people have asked the question: if God created the world, why did he then allow miracles to happen which break the natural laws of the universe?

A 'miracle' is a marvellous event which cannot have been brought about by humans or by nature, and so is said to be performed by God. Usually a miracle shows control over the laws of nature.

There are many instances in the New Testament of Jesus performing miracles: he turned water into wine, he walked on the sea, he healed the sick, raised the dead, and calmed a storm.

The question that miraculous events raise is: would God willingly break the natural laws of the universe which he created? While it could be said that God would of course break the laws if there was sufficient reason, it is difficult to say now that events such as turning water into wine were sufficiently important for him to do so.

Some Christians have argued that it does not matter whether the miracles of the New Testament really happened or not. What is important is the spiritual message about God's love for humanity which lies behind these miracles.

The book of Genesis explains the relationship between God and humans. God created people, but then allowed them to be free agents in their relationship with him and the world:

> Then God said, 'Let us make man in our image, in our likeness, and let them rule over the fish of the sea and the birds of the air, over the livestock, over all the earth, and over all the creatures that move along the ground.' So God created man in his own image, in the image of God he created him; male and female he created them. God blessed them and said to them, 'Be fruitful and increase in number; fill the earth and subdue it. Rule over the fish of the sea and the birds of the air and over every living creature that moves on the ground.'
> (Genesis 1:26–28)

Stephen William Hawking (1942–), British theoretical physicist.

The Qur'an contains the following account of Creation:

> *Your Guardian-Lord is God, who created the heavens and the earth in six days, and is firmly established on the Throne (of authority): He draweth the night as a veil o'er the day, each seeking the other in rapid succession: He created the sun, the moon, and the stars, (all) governed by laws under His Command.*
> *It is He who sendeth the winds… From the land that is clean and good, by the will of its Cherisher, springs up produce, (rich) after its kind.*
>
> (Surah 7:54-58)

The Qur'an does not give a sequence of Creation but it says that Allah created everything. The word which is translated in this extract as 'day' is *ayyam* which means 'long periods' or 'ages'. It would seem that the Qur'an is saying that God created the universe over a long period of time.

The creation of humans is also explained:

> *I have only created Jinns and men, that they may serve me. No sustenance did I require of them, nor do I require that they should feed me. For God is He who gives (all) sustenance,—Lord of Power,— steadfast (for ever).*
>
> (Surah 51:56–58)

Cosmology and evolution

Islam has always been very closely linked to science. Modern theories of cosmology and evolution, therefore, do not create any problems for Muslims. They believe that the Qur'an is the Word of Allah and true and they also believe that Allah is in charge of the world. Science does not challenge their belief that Allah controls everything, but it can explain what is not said in the Qu'ran.

The Qur'an contains some details which are surprising considering that it was written down long before many scientific discoveries were made. The following extract is an account of how the world began:

> *Do not the disbelievers realise that the heavens and earth were a solid mass, then We split them asunder, and We made from water every living thing? …He it is Who created the night and the day, and the sun and the moon each gliding freely in its orbit.*
>
> (Surah 21:31-34)

The extract seems to be saying that life began in what scientists now call the 'primordial soup'. It also shows understanding of the fact that the sun and moon are in particular and separate orbits. Such scientific accuracy made long before scientific discoveries is explained by Muslims as God's way of revealing these things through the Qur'an.

Because the Qur'an contains explanations of life, scientific discoveries are welcomed and accepted by Muslims. They are seen as further explanations of the wonder of Allah's Creation. The arguments about cosmology or evolution do not create any real problems for Muslims. Instead, these theories demonstrate humanity's gradual understanding of what was already revealed to the Prophet Muhammad.

Miracles

Miracles do not play a particularly important part in Islam. Because the Muhammad was a prophet and not seen as a God, there is no reason why he should have performed miracles.

The Qur'an itself is sometimes seen as a living miracle because of the way in which it has been passed on, unchanged, since it was revealed to the Prophet Muhammad.

There was, however, an important miraculous event in the life of the Prophet: the **Al-Mi'raj** – the Ascent. Muhammad was woken by Jibril, the angel, who took him to Jerusalem on an animal with wings, called Buraq. In Jerusalem, Muhammad met the Prophets of Allah: Adam, Ibrahim, Musa, 'Isa and Harun. He then travelled through the heavens until he came into the presence of Allah.

Apart from this event, Islam has few references to miracles in its history. Although it is clear from the Qur'an that Allah is able to perform miracles if he wished, they are not a problem for Muslims in relation to science.

The Qur'an contains details which are scientifically accurate. For example, it explains the passage of water and its role in the growth of life:

> Seest thou not that God sends down rain from the sky, and leads it through springs in the earth? Then He causes to grow, therewith, produce of various colours.
>
> (Surah 39:21)

There is also knowledge of the process of circulation within the body:

> And verily in cattle (too) will ye find an instructive sign. From what is within their bodies, between excretions and blood, we produce, for your drink, milk, pure and agreeable to those who drink it.
>
> (Surah 16:66)

Summary

All three religions have accounts of how the world began. People who believe in their accounts as historical fact, find it difficult to accept modern explanations of Creation and evolution. Today, however, many people of different religious traditions view their scriptures as God's explanation to people of the purposes of life. It is easier, therefore, for them to accept modern scientific explanations of Creation and evolution.

Protesters in anti-pollution suits at a Greenpeace rally.

1 What do you understand by:

Creation

evolution

the Big Bang theory

revelation and truth

miracles

fundamentalist views?

2 Choose one religion and explain in detail how it says Creation took place.

3 Explain the scientific arguments for Creation and evolution.

4 Look at the arguments for Creation and explain whether you think there is any real problem in following a religion and being a scientist.

5 Explain the different ways in which people might understand miracles and their purpose.

6 In what ways might it be true to say that miracles no longer happen?

7 Consider whether scientific discoveries about evolution have damaged religion.

4 Good or bad?

'She's such a good person', people sometimes say, or 'That woman, she's evil.'

What do these expressions mean? How can we say that someone, or something, is 'good' or 'evil' – what do the words themselves mean?

'Good' is something we like, something that is beneficial to us or to others. 'Evil', on the other hand, is not just something that we don't like, it is much stronger. Evil makes people suffer and does them harm.

When we use the words 'right' and 'wrong' we are making judgements about things. This is similar to what happens when we use the words 'good' and 'evil'. We are making judgements based on what we know, or what we think we know, and we are using a set of rules, by which we can judge things for ourselves. Our basic code of rules is, in some ways, very much like the Ten Commandments. Religious people believe that God is the origin of everything that is good. It is God who influences us to behave in the 'right' way.

So what is it that makes people behave in the 'wrong' way? What is it that guides and influences people who we may describe as 'evil'?

Many religions have said that God is a power of good, yet since some people's behaviour could be described as evil, there must also be a power of evil. This is the force which is sometimes referred to as Satan or the devil. Many religious people believe that God influences people to be good and the devil persuades them to be evil. The difference is that although God permits this power of evil to exist, it is God who finally judges us on our lives. If you live according to God's teachings then he will reward you. If you do not, God will punish you.

Many people, however, would say that it is a weakness in humans themselves that causes them to choose not to follow these rules and not the power of evil. Every human being has the choice: they can behave in a way which is positive and good or they can choose a way which may seem good for themselves, but is bad for others.

There are still two questions which we have not answered: if God is good then why does he let evil exist? if God created and loves humans, how can he let 'evil' things happen? The three religions try to answer these questions. As well as this, they also teach how we should treat people who break these rules – with forgiveness.

How do we learn that something is good, evil, right or wrong? From our families and the people around us, we learn a basic set of rules:

> Don't lie
> Don't hurt people
> Don't swear (certainly not when you are young)
> Don't steal
> Do what your parents tell you.

These are just some of the rules that most of us learn, but where do they come from originally? And if these rules are easy and obvious, why do we sometimes break them?

The devil on a wall painting in Mali, Western Africa.

Satan as an evil power does not appear in the Jewish scriptures until the Book of Chronicles where he is seen as influencing King David:

> Satan rose up against Israel and incited David to take a census of Israel.
>
> (1 Chronicles 21:1)

Originally, Jews believed that people were punished for the wrong things which their parents or grandparents had done:

> I, the Lord your God, am a jealous God, punishing the children for the sin of the fathers to the third and fourth generation of those who hate me, but showing love to a thousand generations of those who love me and keep my commandments.
>
> (Exodus 20:5-6)

Later, however, the prophet Ezekiel said that people could only be punished for their own sins:

> 'What do you people mean by quoting this proverb about the land of Israel: "The fathers eat sour grapes, and the children's teeth are set on edge"? As surely as I live, declares the Sovereign Lord, you will no longer quote this proverb in Israel.'
>
> (Ezekiel 18:2-3)

Followers of Judaism believe that when God created humans, he made them so that they could choose whether to worship him or not. This is called **free will**. People must follow God's teachings because they have decided that it is the right thing to do.

If we are free to choose, however, then we will sometimes make mistakes and we will suffer because of this:

> *Not to have known suffering is not to be truly human.*
>
> (Midrash)

In Judaism, the story of humanity and the battle between good and evil begins with the story of Adam and Eve in the Garden of Eden:

> *The Lord God took the man and put him in the Garden of Eden to work it and take care of it. And the Lord God commanded the man, 'You are free to eat from any tree in the garden; but you must not eat from the tree of the knowledge of good and evil, for when you eat of it you will surely die.'*
>
> (Genesis 2:15-17)

> *…a serpent tempted Eve to eat from this tree… She also gave some to her husband, who was with her, and he ate it. Then…they realised that they were naked; so they sewed fig leaves together and made coverings for themselves…and they hid from the Lord God among the trees of the garden. But the Lord God called to the man, 'Where are you?' He answered, 'I heard you in the garden, and I was afraid because I was naked; so I hid.'…Then the Lord God said to the woman, 'What is this you have done?' The woman said, 'The serpent deceived me, and I ate.'…So the Lord God banished Adam from the Garden of Eden to work the ground from which he had been taken. After he drove the man out, he placed on the east side of the Garden of Eden cherubim and a flaming sword flashing back and forth to guard the way to the tree of life.*
>
> (Genesis 3:1-24)

Although the serpent is seen as tempting Adam and Eve to do something evil (something which God did not want them to do), Judaism does not describe the serpent as the devil or Satan.

Jews usually think of Satan as a fallen angel who was punished for challenging God. In the Book of Job, however, he is seen as a sort of spy for God who travels around the earth and reports everyone who he sees behaving against God's wishes. God allows him to do this, but sets limits on his power.

Punishment and forgiveness

The Torah deals with how evil is to be judged and punished. Death is ordered for a number of crimes including killing someone, hitting or cursing your parents, committing adultery, committing incest, kidnap and breaking the Sabbath.

> *While the Israelites were in the desert, a man was found gathering wood on the Sabbath day. Those who found him gathering wood brought him to Moses and Aaron and the whole assembly, and they kept him in custody, because it was not clear what should be done to him. Then the Lord said to Moses, 'The man must die. The whole assembly must stone him outside the camp.' So the assembly took him outside the camp and stoned him to death, as the Lord commanded Moses.*
>
> (Numbers 15:32-36)

Obviously this seems very severe and is not practised by Jews today.

In the Talmud a number of Rabbis argued why they should not order the death penalty. They felt that a **Beth Din** (Jewish Court) which ordered the death penalty once in seventy years was bloodthirsty. Later, they ordered that before an execution two witnesses must have warned the person that what they were going to do carried the death penalty. The two witnesses had to agree that the warning was given and then the crime committed. Also, they decided that if all the judges agreed on the death penalty, then the person must go free as it was probable that the judges were not being unprejudiced. Finally, the judges had to take part in the execution.

Although the Torah does order the death penalty, the State of Israel abolished it in the 1950s. The only crime for which it is kept is for having taken part in the Holocaust. This was the killing of six million Jews by the Nazis during the Second World War. Despite the number of people who have been tried for this crime, however, only one has been executed. Jews are unwilling to take life even though, for many centuries, they have been persecuted by others.

Every year, in preparation for **Yom Kippur**, the Day of Atonement, Jews apologise to everyone they might have upset during the year and they also apologise to God on behalf of everyone for everything they have done wrong during the year. They do not make an individual apology but apologise on behalf of everyone listing all the sins which the Jewish people may have committed:

> *We have become guilty, we have betrayed, we have robbed, we have spoken slander. We have caused perversion, we have caused wickedness, we have sinned wilfully, we have extorted, we have accused falsely. We have given evil counsel, we have been deceitful, we have scorned, we have rebelled, we have provoked, we have turned away, we have been perverse, we have acted wantonly, we have persecuted, we have been obstinate. We have been wicked, we have corrupted, we have been abominable, we have strayed.*

Moses punishing the Israelites for worshipping the golden calf.

33

When a baby is being baptised the Priest says:

> Bless this water, that your servants who are washed in it may be made one with Christ in his death and in his resurrection, to be cleansed and delivered from all sin.

The congregation say:

> Fight valiantly under the banner of Christ against sin, the world, and the devil.
> (Alternative Service Book)

Adam and Eve in the Garden of Eden, *Hironymus Bosch (1450–1516)*.

Christian teaching on good and evil is not a clearly black or white issue – it is not possible just to say things are 'right' or 'wrong'.

Christianity teaches that Adam and Eve sinned in the Garden of Eden by eating the fruit of the Forbidden Tree. Through this act, not only were they disobeying God but also, they were responsible for bringing sin on to human beings. Since that time, all children have been born with original sin (the sin of Adam and Eve) which can only be removed from them by baptism. Until recently, the Roman Catholic Church taught that if a baby died without being baptised, it would spend eternity in limbo and could never enter heaven.

As well as a power of good, Christians believe in a power of evil. It is said that Lucifer, one of the archangels, was guilty of pride in his relationship with God. Because of this, he was thrown out of heaven. He fell to hell where he became Satan, the devil. A reference to this story can be found in Luke's Gospel where Jesus is talking to seventy disciples:

> 'I saw Satan fall like lightning from heaven.'
>
> (Luke 10:18)

Christians believe that God is much stronger than the devil so the power for good is much stronger than the power for evil. God has given people free will, however, so they can choose whether they follow him or not and they are able to decide to do wrong as well as right.

Some Christians believe that the devil can 'possess' people and affect their behaviour. When this happens people, and sometimes buildings, are **exorcised**: prayers are said to remove the devil. Most Christians today, however, do not believe that people can be 'possessed by demons' and that usually there are medical reasons for this type of behaviour.

The work of Jesus

Before Jesus came to earth, people believed that they would be punished for their sins after death by being sent to hell. The death and resurrection of Jesus meant that Christians could be forgiven for their sins.

According to the New Testament, Jesus was put to death by the Romans because he was accused of blasphemy by the Jews.

Jesus was very badly treated by the Romans. He was whipped and a 'crown' of sharp thorns was pushed on to his head. After this he was made to carry his cross from the prison to the place where criminals were executed. Here he was nailed to the cross by his wrists and feet and left to die. During the three hours which he lived, nailed to the cross, he asked God, his father, to forgive the people who punished him:

> 'Father, forgive them, for they do not know what they are doing.'
>
> (Luke 23:34)

Three days after his death, he was seen again by the disciples: Jesus had risen from the dead. This is called the **resurrection**. Jesus lived with the disciples on earth for a further forty days until he finally returned to heaven.

Jesus did not fight against his execution but died innocently and, because of this, the sins of humanity were forgiven: he **atoned** for them. Christians believe that Jesus defeated death and came back to life. From that time forward, people who accept Jesus' teachings and that he is the Son of God, can be assured that when they die, they will be with him in heaven.

On the night before he was put to death, Jesus celebrated the Last Supper with his disciples. At this meal he shared bread and wine with them.

While they were eating, Jesus took bread, gave thanks and broke it, and gave it to his disciples, saying, 'Take and eat; this is my body.' Then he took the cup, gave thanks and offered it to them, saying, 'Drink from it, all of you. This is my blood of the covenant, which is poured out for many for the forgiveness of sins.'

(Matthew 26:26–28)

Christians remember this meal each time they celebrate the Eucharist. By saying these words and sharing bread and wine, they believe that they are bringing Jesus back into their lives and reminding themselves of his atonement for their sins.

Punishment and forgiveness

At the time of Jesus, capital punishment for crimes was an accepted part of life. Although Jesus did not say that the death penalty was wrong, he said many things which suggest that people should be forgiven:

'You have heard that it was said, "Love your neighbour and hate your enemy." But I tell you: Love your enemies and pray for those who persecute you, that you may be sons of your Father in heaven.'

(Matthew 5:43–44)

Jesus was capable of being angry, however, and did become annoyed when people did things which were offensive to God.

Forgiveness and love for other people were at the centre of Christ's teaching and so are at the centre of Christianity:

'Teacher, which is the greatest commandment in the Law?' Jesus replied: 'Love the Lord your God with all your heart and with all your soul and with all your mind. This is the first and greatest commandment. And the second is like it: Love your neighbour as yourself.'

(Matthew 22:36–39)

Jesus was teaching that not only should people follow God's laws but that to forgive one another was one of the most important of these.

Consequently, just as the result of one trespass was condemnation for all men, so also the result of one act of righteousness was justification that brings life for all men. For just as through the disobedience of the one man the many were made sinners, so also through the obedience of the one man the many will be made righteous.

(Romans 5:18-19)

This passage from a letter written by Paul explains how the sin of Adam and Eve was forgiven by Jesus' actions.

An example of Jesus' forgiveness is found in John's Gospel:

The teachers of the law and the Pharisees brought in a woman caught in adultery. They made her stand before the group and said to Jesus, 'Teacher, this woman was caught in the act of adultery. In the Law Moses commanded us to stone such women. Now what do you say?'... he straightened up and said to them, 'If any one of you is without sin, let him be the first to throw a stone at her.' ...At this, those who heard began to go away one at a time, the older ones first, until only Jesus was left, with the woman still standing there. Jesus straightened up and asked her, 'Woman, where are they? Has no one condemned you?' 'No one, sir,' she said. 'Then neither do I condemn you,' Jesus declared. 'Go now and leave your life of sin.'

(John 8:3-11)

A Muslim sins against Allah by not living according to the Five Pillars:

Shahadah	declaration of faith
Salah	five compulsory daily prayers
Zakah	purification of wealth by payment of annual welfare due
Hajj	pilgrimage to Makkah
Sawm	fasting during Ramadan

It is Allah who decides whether someone will be punished or forgiven. Muslims do not make public confessions of their sins.

According to the Qur'an Adam and Hawwa' (Eve) were tempted by Shaytan and ate the fruit of the forbidden tree in Al-Jannah (Paradise). Allah forgave Adam and Hawwa' their sins when they prayed to him:

'Our Lord! we have wronged our own souls: If Thou forgive us not and bestow not upon us Thy mercy, we shall certainly be lost.'

(Surah 7:23)

Allah said:

'Get ye down all from here; And if, as is sure, there comes to you guidance from Me, whosoever follows My guidance, on them shall be no fear, nor shall they grieve.'

(Surah 2:38)

A cutting from The Observer *newspaper, 1978*

Muslims believe that all human beings are born without sin (fitrah). Muslims have free will and can choose whether to follow the will of Allah (Islam) or to choose to do wrong.

Allah forgives people who acknowledge that they are wrong and pray for forgiveness. Islam teaches that goodness is always better than evil:

Nor can goodness and evil be equal. Repel (evil) with that which is better.

(Surah 41:34)

It teaches that Allah made **Mala'ikah** (angels) from **nur** (divine light); he created Adam, the first human, from clay; he also created spirits called **Jinn** and these came from fire. After Allah had made Adam, he ordered the angels and Jinn to bow down to his new creation. The angels obeyed but Iblis (the devil) a Jinn, refused.

(God) said: 'O Iblis! what is your reason For not being among those who prostrated themselves?' (Iblis) said: 'I am not one to prostrate myself to man, whom Thou didst create from sounding clay, from mud moulded into shape.' (God) said: 'Then get thee out from here; for thou are rejected, accursed. And the curse shall be on thee till the Day of Judgement.'

(Surah 15:32–35)

Iblis said that he would tempt humans for ever to choose wrong rather than right. Iblis is sometimes called Shaytan (the devil). In his last sermon, Prophet Muhammad warned his followers:

Beware of Shaytan, he is desperate to divert you from the worship of Allah, so beware of him in matters of your religion.

Islam says that during their lives, people will be tempted. Life is a series of tests to which people have to find their own solutions:

Be sure we shall test you With something of fear And hunger, some loss In goods or lives or the fruits (of your toil), but give Glad tidings to those who patiently persevere,—who say, when afflicted with calamity: 'To God we belong, and to Him is our return':—They are those on whom (Descend) blessings from God and Mercy, and they are the ones that receive guidance.

(Surah 2:155–157)

WORLD THIS WEEK

Why Saudis cling to Islam's harshest code

by ROBERT STEPHENS, our Diplomatic Correspondent

THE public caning of two Britons in Saudi Arabia has focused attention on the traditional Islamic legal code known as the Sharia, and revealed much confusion about its role in Muslim and Arab countries.

gan in the last century under the Ottoman Empire and under European imperial administrations.

At the same time, Islam was going through an attempted reformation to adapt itself to the modern world.

At the other extreme were traditionalists reacted to

rulers have sought to play a more active role in the political leadership of the Arab world.

To this end they have used the combination of their oil wealth and their prestige in Islam as guardians of the Holy Places.

Inside the country there have been conflicting trends

Shaytan is not equal to Allah, however, and although he is used to test a Muslim's faith, he cannot harm people unless Allah permits it:

…(Shaytan) cannot harm them in the least, except as God permits; and on God let the believers put their trust.

(Surah 58:10)

Punishment and forgiveness

Shari'ah, Islamic law, is based on the Qur'an.

Shari'ah is clear that a murderer should be killed. However, the victim's family can decide to take money or goods from the murderer rather than their life. This covers cases of manslaughter where the death was unintentional.

O ye who believe! The law of equality is prescribed to you in cases of murder: the free for the free, the slave for the slave, the woman for the woman. But if any remission is made by the brother of the slain, then grant any reasonable demand, And compensate him with handsome gratitude. This is a concession and a mercy from your Lord after this whoever exceeds the limits shall be in grave penalty.

(Surah 2:178)

If someone murders a person without good cause:

…if any one slew a person — unless it be for murder or for spreading mischief in the land — it would be as if he slew the whole people.

(Surah 5:35)

There are penalties for thieves and murderers:

The punishment of those who wage war against God and His Apostle, and strive with might and main for mischief through the land is: execution, or crucifixion, or the cutting off of hands and feet from opposite sides, or exile from the land: that is their disgrace in this world, and a heavy punishment is theirs in the hereafter; except for those who repent before they fall into your power.

(Surah 5:36–37)

Allah is a merciful, forgiving ruler and judge and Muslims are required to follow this example:

Hold to forgiveness; command what is right; but turn away from the ignorant.

(Surah 7:199)

Those who are kind and considerate to Allah's creatures, Allah bestows His kindness and affection on them.

(Abu Dawud, Tirmidhi)

Muslims, therefore, must follow the will of Allah and also follow his example of forgiveness to others.

Shari'ah has strict rules and procedures for these cases of murder and theft:

- *people must be tried by a legal court*
- *murder during a robbery is punished by death*
- *bodily harm during a robbery is punished by cutting off a hand and a foot*
- *less serious crimes are punished by prison sentences*

37

Summary

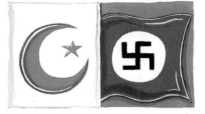

From this chapter we can see that each of these religions has similar views on the relationship between good and evil and the way in which God thinks people should behave. They all believe that God is good and the power of goodness.

Each of them also has a belief in a power of evil which is sometimes described as a person.

In addition, although these religions may have harsh penalties for certain crimes, each of them has a way in which people can show forgiveness and soften the penalties.

The Fall of Lucifer,
Queen Mary's Psalter,
(14th century)

1 What do you understand by:

   natural disaster

   good and evil

   right and wrong

   forgiveness

   atonement

   punishment?

2 How can we decide whether something or someone is good or evil?

3 Consider whether there are some sins or crimes which cannot be forgiven.

4 How would you explain the fact that religious people can die in natural disasters?

5 Do you think that it is possible for a member of one of these religions to order the death of another person?

6 In your opinion, is it possible that the devil is a real person, or do you think that it is natural for people to choose to behave wrongly?

7 If God really is good, why do you think that he allows evil to exist? Should he make all people behave well?

5 Prayer, worship and the 'Holy Other'

Spirituality is a difficult word to explain and to understand. The dictionary says that spirituality means:

The quality or condition of being spiritual; attachment to or regard for things of the spirit as opposed to material or worldly interests.

It deals with ideas and feelings people have sometimes which cannot be described in a 'normal' way.

You might be standing on a cliff by the sea in a strong wind and feel a sense of excitement. You might get a special feeling when you hear a particular piece of music. You might also get a special feeling when you walk into a religious building. It is difficult to put these feelings into words. We might try to by using expressions such as 'a sense of awe' or 'a sense of wonder'. We are experiencing something which we cannot explain.

Many religious people would say that we are having a religious experience – we are feeling something which is different from the ordinary sensations which we have every day.

For some people, a spiritual feeling gives them certainty in their faith – they feel that they 'know' God exists because they have this feeling.

People express their spiritual feelings in different ways:

Prayer

This does not necessarily mean asking for anything for themselves, it could be asking God to intervene in the world and, perhaps, help someone who is ill. Prayer could simply be thanking God for something.

Meditation

People may sit quietly and try to empty their minds of ordinary thought and, they would say, listen to their spiritual feelings.

Religious services

Others may express spirituality by attending religious services, while some people will see their whole life and their relationships with other people as a spiritual experience.

There are different ways in which people express spirituality: in art; religious buildings; in music, and in religious ceremonies and liturgy (the way in which people worship).

As well as these ways of expressing spirituality, spiritual beliefs and feelings are expressed in the sacred writings of religions and how they are regarded and treated.

The way in which spirituality is expressed varies between religions.

The cathedral of Sagrada Familia (Sacred Family) by Antoni Gaudi y Cornet in Barcelona, Spain.

A German theologian called Rudolf Otto (1869-1937) believed that when we have a sense of wonder and awe, we are experiencing God. He called this feeling the 'Holy Other' and used the word **numinous** to describe the presence of God which inspires awe and reverence - something which is holy and totally different from any other experience.

Jews believe in God as being **omnipotent** (all powerful) and **omniscient** (all knowing). This belief is found in the teachings of the Tenakh:

> I saw the Lord seated on a throne, high and exalted, and the train of his robe filled the temple. Above him were seraphs, each with six wings: With two wings they covered their faces, with two they covered their feet, and with two they were flying. And they were calling to one another: 'Holy, holy, holy is the Lord Almighty; the whole earth is full of his glory.'
> At the sound of their voices the doorposts and thresholds shook and the temple was filled with smoke.
>
> (Isaiah 6:1-4)

Jews are born into Judaism (everyone who has a Jewish mother is considered to be a Jew) and so may follow God's will as an expression of their spirituality. This will is contained in the Ten Commandments and is stated in the Shema (see page 16).

Spirituality is expressed in every aspect of Jewish life as Jews follow the **613 mitzvot** or Commandments which are found in the Torah. These Commandments give rules for many parts of life including clothing, food, sexual relations, and prayer and worship.

Many Jewish ceremonies are based in the home and the family, but originally the Temple in Jerusalem was at the centre of Jewish life and worship in Israel. The Temple was first built by King Solomon and then rebuilt by Herod the Great. Here, people offered daily sacrifices according to the rules in the Torah. Also, the Ark of the Covenant was kept here. It contained the tablets of stone on which Moses had written the Ten Commandments.

Many attempts were made by other nations to take the Temple and there are stories of the Jews fighting to keep it. It was finally destroyed by the armies of the Roman Empire in 70 CE and has not been rebuilt. As the House of God it had provided a focus for Jews where prayer and worship could be centralised. Following its destruction, worship turned to the home and to the synagogues which are found in Jewish communities all over the world. No sacrifices can be performed in a synagogue but they contain the Sefer Torah, copies of the scrolls of the Torah.

Worship in the synagogue and at home

Jews pray at least three times a day:

    Shacharit – dawn
    Minchah – afternoon
    Maariv – evening

Jewish men go to the synagogue to pray and to hear the reading of the Torah. Services are held every day. The most important time for these services is the Sabbath, on Friday evenings and Saturday mornings.

The synagogue is usually a plain building. The main room or sanctuary is an area of seats which face the east wall. This wall faces Jerusalem and bears the **Aron Hakodesh**, the ark which contains the scrolls of the Torah. These are covered by a door or a curtain and often have richly decorated mantles or covers. They also have a **rimmonim** (bells) and a breastplate which represents one worn by the High Priest in the Temple. There are no statues, pictures or photographs in the sanctuary because of the following commandment:

'You shall not make for yourself an idol in the form of anything in heaven above or on the earth beneath or in the waters below. You shall not bow down to them or worship them; for I, the Lord your God, am a jealous God.'

(Exodus 20:4-5)

Often there is a seven-branched candlestick called a **menorah**. This represents the candlestick which is said to have been in the Temple. There will also be a **bimah** or platform from which the Torah is read. Orthodox synagogues have a gallery for the women, or a partition which they sit behind. In Progressive synagogues, men and women sit together.

A service in an Orthodox synagogue.

Worship in a synagogue is lead by a **chazan** who will sing much of the service. Although most synagogues have an organ, in Orthodox services the singing is always unaccompanied on the Sabbath because playing musical instruments is considered to be work. In Progressive synagogues the organ may be used.

The Torah is always read in Hebrew, the ancient language of the Jews. In Progressive synagogues some of the prayers said during the service may be in English, but all Orthodox services and prayers are in Hebrew.

Although the synagogue is important to Jews, the main place of worship remains in the home and within the family. Here the many food laws have to be carried out. On Friday evenings, a special meal is prepared for the Sabbath. Two candles are lit to welcome the Sabbath into the house. At the end of the Sabbath the service of Havdalah is performed as the new week begins. Worship within the home reminds people of the importance of the family in Jewish life.

Sacred texts

Jews believe that the Torah is the word of God and that it should be written and read in its original language. However, the scriptures are available in many languages so that people can study them and those who cannot read Hebrew can still understand them.

Art and architecture

Judaism is an ancient religion and, since the destruction of the Temple, Jews have lived all over the world in the **Diaspora**. As a result, Jewish culture is very rich and has been influenced by the places where Jews have settled. Jewish spirituality, therefore, is expressed in many ways through music, art and the architecture and design of synagogues.

The Holy Spirit came to the first disciples on the Festival of Pentecost, just after Jesus' ascension into heaven.

> When the day of Pentecost came, they were all together in one place. Suddenly a sound like the blowing of a violent wind came from heaven and filled the whole house where they were sitting. They saw what seemed to be tongues of fire that separated and came to rest on each of them. All of them were filled with the Holy Spirit and began to speak in other tongues as the Spirit enabled them.
>
> (Acts 2:1-4)

This is the Spirit which Jesus promised would come to the disciples after he had left them and gone to heaven:

> 'When the Counsellor comes, whom I will send to you from the Father, the Spirit of truth who goes out from the Father, he will testify about me.'
>
> (John 15:26)

The 'Jesus Prayer'
Lord Jesus, Son of God
be merciful to me, a sinner.

The Hail Mary
Hail Mary, full of grace,
the Lord is with thee.
Blessed art thou among women
and blessed is the fruit of the womb, Jesus.
Holy Mary, Mother of God,
pray for us sinners, now, and at the hour of our death. Amen.

For many Christians, their spirituality is centred on the Church. This does not mean a church building, but the group of people who form it. This idea of the Church and its members is shown in the Apostles' Creed:

> I believe in… the holy Catholic Church, the communion of saints.

Christians believe that the Church is guided by the **Holy Spirit**. The Holy Spirit is the third person, or part, of the Christian Trinity.

The Holy Spirit is first shown in the New Testament when Jesus is baptised:

> When all the people were being baptised, Jesus was baptised too. And as he was praying, heaven was opened and the Holy Spirit descended on him in bodily form like a dove. And a voice came from heaven: 'You are my Son, whom I love; with you I am well pleased.'
>
> (Luke 3:21-22)

A vision of the fall of angels, *Hildegaard of Bingen (1098–1179)*

This Spirit continues to guide the Christian Church today. When the Roman Catholic Church chooses a new Pope, for example, it asks the Holy Spirit for guidance. The Cardinals (the most senior members of the Church) sit in a room with the door sealed; they pray that the Holy Spirit will guide them to know who God has chosen as the next Pope.

Worship

Christians believe that when they worship they may receive guidance from the Holy Spirit. This worship takes many different forms. Sometimes Christians pray privately. They may use this opportunity just to talk to God or they may use particular prayers. Three of the best known prayers are the The Lord's Prayer which Jesus taught to his disciples (Matthew 6:9-15), The 'Jesus Prayer', and the Hail Mary.

As well as prayer, many Churches use special forms of services, called **liturgy**, in their worship. Most liturgies celebrate the Eucharist – a celebration of the Last Supper which Jesus had with his disciples before his crucifixion. This is also called Breaking of bread, Holy Communion, Lord's Supper, Mass, and other names.

Many people believe that this ceremony is a symbolic repeating of what Jesus did at the Last Supper. Others, such as Roman Catholics, believe in a teaching called **transubstantiation**. This means that the bread and wine become the actual body and blood of Jesus when the priest repeats Jesus' words.

Some Christians spend time thinking about God by meditating. They sit quietly and try to clear their minds of ordinary thoughts so that they can 'hear' what God has to say to them. Another form of Christian worship is called **charismatic**. People try to 'open' themselves to the Holy Spirit. Often the result of this kind of worship is **glossolalia** (speaking in tongues). People believe that the Holy Spirit has entered them and, like the first disciples at Pentecost, they begin to pray and praise God in languages which they themselves cannot speak or understand:

Now there were staying in Jerusalem God-fearing Jews from every nation under heaven. When they heard this sound, a crowd came together in bewilderment, because each one heard them speaking in his own language. Utterly amazed, they asked: 'Are not all these men who are speaking Galileans? Then how is it that each of us hears them in his own native language? Parthians, Medes and Elamites; residents of Mesopotamia, Judea and Cappadocia, Pontus and Asia, Phrygia and Pamphylia, Egypt and the parts of Libya near Cyrene; visitors from Rome (both Jews and converts to Judaism); Cretans and Arabs–we hear them declaring the wonders of God in our own tongues!'

(Acts 2:5–11)

Art and architecture

Christian spirituality is also expressed in the art, architecture and music of the Church. Christianity has probably been the major influence on all European forms of art. Many of the greatest artists of the last thousand years have painted religious pictures based on Christianity. Every European town has Christian buildings which are often a very important part of the architecture there. As well as this, all the great composers have written religious music. Sometimes this has been hymns or choral music, but many have also composed instrumental music inspired by Christian teachings and belief.

Sacred texts

Christians believe that the Bible is the most sacred book because it contains the Word of God and stories about Jesus and his teachings. It is so important to them that it has been translated into almost every language in the world so that everyone can have the opportunity to learn about Christianity.

All these expressions of spirituality show Christians' belief in God. The art, architecture, music and liturgy of Christianity are all designed to praise God and to show the holiness of God.

The Eucharist may be a very simple event with a person reading Jesus' words from the Bible before sharing bread and wine with the other people present:

'For I received from the Lord what I also passed on to you: The Lord Jesus, on the night he was betrayed, took bread, and when he had given thanks, he broke it and said, "This is my body, which is for you; do this in remembrance of me." In the same way, after supper he took the cup, saying, "This cup is the new covenant in my blood; do this, whenever you drink it, in remembrance of me." For whenever you eat this bread and drink this cup, you proclaim the Lord's death until he comes.'

(1 Corinthians 11:23–26)

It may be a very elaborate ceremony with music and singing. There may be several priests wearing special clothes (vestments) and many prayers may be said before and after the central repeating of Jesus' words.

Some Christians feel that the only way in which they can express their true spirituality is through devoting their whole life to God without any secular distractions. In order to do this, they live in convents or monasteries as nuns or monks. They often have very little to do with the outside world. Instead, they spend their time in prayer and adopt a very simple lifestyle.

In this life they take their vows:

Poverty:	*they have no personal possessions*
Chastity:	*they do not have any sexual relationships*
Obedience:	*they agree to follow the instructions of the leader of the community in which they live*

The Five Pillars

At the centre of Islamic life and belief are the Five Pillars:

- *Shahadah: the declaration of faith which states 'There is no god except Allah, Muhammad (pbuh) is the Messenger of Allah'. The declaration itself is the Kalimah Tayyibah and within it is the whole of Muslim belief.*
- *Salah: five compulsory daily prayers for communicating with, and worshipping Allah. These are performed under specific conditions, in the manner taught by the Prophet Muhammad and are said in Arabic.*
  The prayers are said at fixed times and can be performed alone or with other people. The five set times during which these can be said are:
  Fajr – from dawn until just before sunset
  Zuhr – after mid-day until afternoon
  'Asr – from late afternoon until just before sunset
  Maghrib – after unset until daylight ends
  'Isha' – night until midnight or dawn

Muslims express their spirituality in many ways. 'Islam' means submission to the will of Allah and it is by living according to his will that Muslims demonstrate their belief.

One of the major demonstrations of Islamic spirituality lies in Shari'ah. This is living according to Muslim law. In countries where the government is Muslim, the whole of the legal system is based on Shari'ah. Shari'ah itself is formed from the teachings and instruction found in the Qur'an and Sunnah.

Sacred texts

All Muslim worship takes place in Arabic. This was the language of the Prophet Muhammad and the Qur'an was received and written in Arabic. All prayer is said in Arabic and Muslims have a duty to learn the language so that they can understand, worship and read the Qur'an. Unlike most other sacred writings, the Qur'an is not translated into other languages. It is permitted to make a version of it in non-Arabic languages but it is believed that these cannot be accurate. In order to fully understand Islam and Allah's will, it is necessary to learn to understand it in Arabic.

Worship in the mosque

The **masjid** (place of prostration) or mosque, is the central place of worship for Muslims. Muslim men gather there for Salat-ul-Jumu'ah midday prayer on Fridays and listen to the Khutbah or speech given by the **Imam** (prayer leader).

Hagia Sophia, Istanbul. Now a mosque.

In the Qur'an rules are given about the mosque:

The mosques of God shall be visited and maintained by such as believe in God and the last Day, establish regular prayers, and practise regular charity, and fear none (at all) except God.

(Surah 9:18)

A mosque belongs to Allah and cannot be owned by any individual or organisation. In the same way, a mosque cannot be sold, mortgaged or rented.

Many mosques are very beautiful buildings. Their design may vary from place to place and from one country to another, but there are certain features which all mosques must have:

- **Prayer hall:** The main open space in the mosque is the prayer hall. One wall must face the Ka'bah in Makkah. A mihrab or niche in the wall shows Muslims the direction in which they must face when they pray. In addition, there is a platform or minbar which the Imam stands on to give the Khutbah. There will be a separate area for women to pray and this is behind a curtain or screen so that they will not distract the men.
- **Minaret** (mosque tower): Most mosques have at least one minaret from which the Adhan or 'call to prayer' is made. A dome represents the heavens and God's Creation.
- **Facilities for wudu:** Mosques have facilities with running water so that people can perform wudu.

Mosques are usually very simple buildings and yet the walls may be highly decorated with verses from the Qur'an, the name and attributes of Allah, and the name of the Prophet Muhammad in Arabic calligraphy. Mosques have no pictures, statues or photographs showing living beings because this would be against the teaching of Islam.

No music is used in Muslim worship. Many Muslims would say that no music is permitted at all within Islam. The Qur'an says:

But there are, among men, those who purchase idle tales, without knowledge (or meaning), to mislead (men) from the Path of God and throw ridicule (on the Path): for such there will be a humiliating penalty.

(Surah 31:6)

Music is seen as one of these 'idle diversions'. Also, the Prophet Muhammad warned:

…there will be (at some future time) people from my Ummah (nation) who will seek to make lawful …the use of musical instruments.

(Sahih Al-Bukhari)

Before prayer Muslims must clean themselves by performing **wudu.** *In order, they wash their hands, mouth, nose, face, arms, head, ears and feet.*
They are then ready to repeat the set prayers.

- **Zakah:** *the purification of wealth by the payment of an annual welfare due. Muslims pay 2 per cent of their savings each year. This keeps wealth free of greed and selfishness and encourages people to be honest. Also, Muslims are urged to make additional voluntary payments called Sadaqah.*

- **Hajj:** *the annual pilgrimage to Makkah, which each Muslim must carry out at least once in a lifetime if he or she has the health and wealth. A Muslim man who has completed Hajj is called Hajji, and a woman, Hajjah. The pilgrimage is made during Dhul Hijjah, the twelfth month.*

- **Sawm:** *fasting from just before dawn until sunset during the month of Ramadan, the ninth month. Muslims must abstain from all food and drink (including water) as well as smoking and sexual relations.*

The fulfilment of these Five Pillars is the duty of every Muslim as a demonstration of their obedience to God's wishes. These five actions are all **Ibadah** – acts of worship which are performed with the intention to obey Allah.

Summary

Spirituality is a vital part of all these religions, but each religion expresses it in different ways. In every instance, however, it is an attempt by believers to demonstrate their love for God and to express that love and their experience of God.

Salome with the head of John the Baptist, Titian (1485–1576)

1 What do you understand by:

  spirituality

  worship

  prayer

  liturgy

  numinous

  awe and wonder

  guidance?

2 Try to explain how people may feel when they are experiencing the numinous.

3 Explain how you think a believer in either Islam or Judaism or Christianity might feel when they pray to God.

4 Look at what followers of each religion believe about their place of worship. Explain its importance and how the particular features and furnishings of the building show this.

5 Consider the views of each religion about its sacred texts and explain why they have different attitudes towards the language of these.

6 How far would you agree that the most important aspect of religion is prayer and that as long as people pray to God, it does not matter how they do it?

7 Find out why, although there are monks and nuns in Christianity, there are none in Islam or Judaism.

6 *But it's not fair*

How often have you heard someone say 'But it's not fair'? How often have you said it yourself? 'It's not fair' is used to describe almost any situation regardless of its importance: it rains when you want to go out, a close friend dies, a tornado kills a hundred people, a woman is paid less than a man for doing the same work.

The Oxford English Dictionary says that 'fair' is used to describe something which is free from bias, fraud, or injustice; so it would seem that 'fair' really means reasonable.

Often when we use the word 'fair' we mean that we do not like what has happened, it seems unreasonable, yet in many cases, it is just that things are not quite as we wanted them.

Sometimes, however it is rather more serious.

Prejudice and discrimination

Thousands of people in the world still suffer from forms of discrimination and prejudice. These may be based on such issues as race, colour, religion, language, sex, sexuality, disability and social class. The discrimination takes the form of some people who have power, exercising that power over people who do not. A simple formula for this is:

Discrimination = Prejudice + Power

Prejudice is an idea or feeling which one person holds and which affects another person. **Discrimination** is when they act on this prejudice and treat the other person badly.

The most severe physical suffering – death – can be a result of war. Most people would probably agree that war is wrong, but there are two theories which are sometimes used to defend or even support war: Holy War and Just War. A Just War is one which is fought according to certain conditions:

1 it must be fought by a legal authority e.g. a government
2 the cause must be just
3 there must be the intention to establish good or correct evil
4 there must be a reasonable chance of success
5 it must be the last resort
6 only sufficient force must be used and civilians should not be involved

Holy War is the idea that sometimes it is necessary to use physical violence in order to defend religion.

The first two articles of the United Nations Declaration of Human Rights state:

Article 1. All human beings are born free and equal in dignity and rights. They are endowed with reason and conscience and should act towards one another in a spirit of brotherhood.
Article 2. Everyone is entitled to all the rights and freedoms set forth in this Declaration, without distinction of any kind, such as race, colour, sex, language, religion, political or other opinion, national or social origin, property, birth or other status.

The Battle of the Somme, *Richard Caton Woodville, (1856–1927)*

This passage from Isaiah shows the hope for peace:

> In the last days the mountain of the Lord's temple will be established as chief among the mountains; it will be raised above the hills, and all nations will stream to it. Many peoples will come and say, 'Come, let us go up to the mountain of the Lord, to the house of the God of Jacob. He will teach us his ways, so that we may walk in his paths.' The law will go out from Zion, the word of the Lord from Jerusalem. He will judge between the nations and will settle disputes for many peoples. They will beat their swords into ploughshares and their spears into pruning hooks. Nation will not take up sword against nation, nor will they train for war any more.
>
> (Isaiah 2:2-4)

The struggle for peace and justice lies at the centre of Judaism:

> *The world endures on three things – justice, truth and peace*
>
> (Ethics of the Fathers 1:18)

Indeed 'shalom', meaning peace, is a word used in Hebrew to mean both 'hello' and 'goodbye'.

There is a phrase in the Torah which has led some people to think that Judaism is based on revenge:

> *But if there is serious injury, you are to take life for life, eye for eye, tooth for tooth, hand for hand, foot for foot.*
>
> (Exodus 21:23-24)

This is called **Lex Talionis** (the law of retaliation). It does not mean that if someone cuts off your hand then you should cut off theirs, however. It was written to limit revenge and says that if someone cuts off your hand then you *must not cut off any more* than their hand. You may think that this is cruel, but we should remember that we are talking about religious teachings which are nearly four thousand years old.

War and peace

Throughout the Jewish scriptures there are examples of wars. Some of the wars described were Holy Wars where the Jews tried to maintain their religion. Others were perhaps Just Wars.

Judaism says that there are three kinds of wars which must be fought:

- **milchemet mitzvah:** war commanded by God – this is similar to a Holy War. Two such wars are described in the Hebrew Bible: the campaign against Amalek, and Joshua and the Israelites' fight for the Promised Land:

  > *Moses my servant is dead. Now then, you and all these people, get ready to cross the Jordan River into the land I am about to give to them – to the Israelites. I will give you every place where you set your foot, as I promised Moses.*
  >
  > (Joshua 1:2-3)

- **milchemet reshut:** optional war – this is what would be described as a Just War.
- **a pre-emptive war** – this may only be fought when an attack upon Israel is imminent. This happened in 1967, when Israel attacked the airfields of Egypt and Syria in the Six Day War to try to prevent a long and bloody siege.

Jews are obliged to protect themselves and other Jews, as well as going to the aid of other countries to prevent the spread of war.

Prejudice and discrimination

The Jewish experience of pogroms over many centuries, and of the 20th-century Holocaust, should make them especially aware of prejudice, discrimination and persecution. Jews believe that they should forgive other people, but that they cannot forgive on behalf of others. When he was asked if he could forgive the Nazis for the Holocaust, Rabbi Hugo Gryn, a Holocaust survivor said that only God could forgive their crimes. Judaism still thinks of most wars as wrong.

The entrance gates of Auschwitz, Poland.

> *Turn from evil and do good; seek peace and pursue it.*
>
> (Psalm 34:14)

Judaism also teaches that wars must be fought properly and humanely:

> *If your enemy is hungry, give him food to eat; if he is thirsty, give him water to drink.*
>
> (Proverbs 25:21)

Another form of discrimination is **sexism**. Some people say that the traditional Jewish attitude towards women is sexist. In Orthodox Judaism, women sit separately from men in synagogue services and cannot take part. Only men are bound by the 613 mitzvot (laws).

Some people claim that this attitude dates back to the punishment of Eve in the Garden of Eden when she picked the fruit of the Tree of Knowledge and gave it to Adam:

> *To the woman he said, 'I will greatly increase your pains in childbearing; with pain you will give birth to children. Your desire will be for your husband, and he will rule over you.'*
>
> (Genesis 3:16)

Progressive Jews believe that the scriptures should be interpreted for the 20th century and so they make no distinction between the way in which men and women are treated. They pray and worship together and women can become rabbis. Jewish teaching about how other people should be treated is very clear:

> *When an alien lives with you in your land, do not ill-treat him. The alien living with you must be treated as one of your native-born. Love him as yourself, for you were aliens in Egypt. I am the Lord your God.*
>
> (Leviticus 19:33–34)

Jews say that all people should follow their own religion and in doing so, they will please God. They believe, however, that everyone should follow the Noachide Code, the Seven Commandments given to Noah by God after the flood.

Jews believe that although they have their own religion, they should work in every way possible to help other people.

At the Sabbath service on Friday night, husbands tell their wife how valuable she is to them:

> A wife of noble character who can find? She is worth far more than rubies. Her husband has full confidence in her and lacks nothing of value. She brings him good, not harm, all the days of her life. ... She watches over the affairs of her household and does not eat the bread of idleness. Her children arise and call her blessed; her husband also, and he praises her: 'Many women do noble things, but you surpass them all.' Charm is deceptive, and beauty is fleeting; but a woman who fears the Lord is to be praised.
>
> (Proverbs 31:10-31)

The Noachide Code

- *Worship only God*
- *Do not blaspheme*
- *Do not murder*
- *Do not steal*
- *Do not commit adultery*
- *Do not be cruel to animals*
- *Establish a system of law and order so that everyone can live together in harmony.*

49

Christianity teaches that all people are equal and that no one is superior or better in God's eyes than anyone else. For a person to make someone suffer or feel inferior for any reason is to break one of the Commandments given by Jesus:

You shall love your neighbour as yourself.

(Matthew 22:39)

Jesus taught that it was essential for people to love others and that, if such love could be found, then humanity would be saved from bitter struggles and wars.

I give you a new commandment, that you love one another. Just as I have loved you, you also should love one another.

(John 13:34)

There are many examples in the history of the Christian Church where this teaching has been ignored. During the Crusades thousands of people were killed in the name of religion; one of the worst slaughters in history took place when attempts were made to force the peoples of South America to become Christians and in the 20th century, Christian countries have fought each other, and non-Christian countries.

War and peace

During the two World Wars some Christians, especially Quakers, were 'conscientious objectors'. They refused to fight, but were often right at the front of the battle working as medical orderlies or ambulance drivers.

Dietrich Bonhoeffer was a German Christian who was killed by the Nazis for helping Jews to escape from concentration camps, and for his part in a plot to assassinate Adolf Hitler. Bonhoeffer saw it as his duty to put to an end the evils of Nazi Germany. He saw the treatment of the Jews by his fellow Germans as an abomination. He joined the Abwehr, a group which planned to assassinate Hitler and in 1945, he was hung for treason. Although he was planning to kill another human being he is still called a pacifist.

Even in the case of war, Christians believe that they should forgive other people who have injured them.

Then Peter came to Jesus and asked, 'Lord, how many times shall I forgive my brother when he sins against me? Up to seven times?' Jesus answered, 'I tell you, not seven times, but seventy-seven times.'

(Matthew 18:21-22)

Seventy-seven times is a number used here to represent the idea that Christians should always forgive.

Jesus taught:

Blessed are the peacemakers, for they will be called children of God.

(Matthew 5.9)

There are only two occasions when Jesus appears to be angry and to take action himself: one was when he cursed a fig tree which was not bearing fruit, the other when he threw the money-changers out of the Temple in Jerusalem:

Jesus entered the temple area and drove out all who were buying and selling there. He overturned the tables of the money-changers and the benches of those selling doves. 'It is written,' he said to them, 'My house will be called a "house of prayer", but you are making it a "den of robbers".'

(Matthew 21:12-13)

When Peter tries to stop Jesus being arrested in the Garden of Gethsemane, Jesus prevents him:

With that, one of Jesus' companions reached for his sword, drew it out and struck the servant of the high priest, cutting off his ear. 'Put your sword back in its place,' Jesus said to him, 'for all who draw the sword will die by the sword.'

(Matthew 26:51-52)

And he touched the man's ear and healed him.

(Luke 22:51)

BUT IT'S NOT FAIR

Prejudice and discrimination

Christianity is opposed to all forms of prejudice and discrimination.

The Christian Church itself has been guilty of racism and intolerance and sometimes people have preached God's message at the expense of local communities and colonies. This was the case in South Africa for many years where the Dutch Reformed Church taught that black people were inferior to the whites; during times of colonisation Christians killed the native people or forced them to convert to Christianity, and many Christians were slave-owners in the American Deep South.

Many Christians today believe that people should have the right to practise their own religion but they also believe that only Christianity has the complete truth about God:

Jesus answered, 'I am the way and the truth and the life. No-one comes to the Father except through me.'

(John 14:6)

The New Catechism of the Roman Catholic Church states that 'the Church still has the obligation and also the sacred right to evangelise all men'.

Paul's teaching about how Christians should treat other people is very straightforward:

From one man he made every nation of men, that they should inhabit the whole earth; and he determined the times set for them and the exact places where they should live.

(Acts 17:26)

There is neither Jew nor Greek, slave nor free, male nor female, for you are all one in Christ Jesus.

(Galatians 3:28)

The Christian Church has sometimes been accused of sexism. The language of the Church has been in favour of men – God is referred to as male. Because some Christians take what the Bible says very literally, and as having absolute authority, passages such as 'God made Man in his own image' are often used against those who demand greater equality in the Church and in society as a whole.

The Bible was written in times very different from now when this was a normal way of seeing the different roles of men and women. The Church is slow to change and many of its old ideas and prejudices still exist. In the Anglican Church in the USA, women have been eligible for ordination for some years, as they have in Canada and New Zealand. However, the Church of England did not permit women to be ordained until 1994. Women priests have been welcomed by many people but others have left the Church of England and have joined the Roman Catholic Church.

We all long for Heaven where God is, but we have it in our power to be in Heaven with Him at this very moment. But being happy with Him now means:
Loving as He loves,
Helping as He helps,
Giving as He gives,
Serving as He serves,
Rescuing as He rescues,
Being with Him twenty-four hours,
Touching him in his distressing disguise.

(Mother Theresa)

Paul says that women are to be quiet in church and keep their heads covered:

Women should remain silent in the churches. They are not allowed to speak, but must be in submission, as the Law says. If they want to enquire about something, they should ask their own husbands at home; for it is disgraceful for a woman to speak in the church.
(1 Corinthians 14:34-35)

Now I want you to realise that the head of every man is Christ, and the head of the woman is man, and the head of Christ is God. Every man who prays or prophesies with his head covered dishonours his head. And every woman who prays or prophesies with her head uncovered dishonours her head—it is just as though her head were shaved. If a woman does not cover her head, she should have her hair cut off; and if it is a disgrace for a woman to have her hair cut or shaved off, she should cover her head. A man ought not to cover his head, since he is the image and glory of God; but the woman is the glory of man.
(1 Corinthians 11:3-7)

Malcolm X (1925-65), leader of the black Muslim movement in the USA.

Like Christianity, Islam sees itself as the only true religion and Muslims believe that they have a duty to lead other people into the faith.

> Strongest among men in enmity to the believers wilt thou find the Jews and Pagans; and nearest among them in love to the believers wilt thou find those who say, 'We are Christians'.
>
> (Surah 5:85)

> If anyone desires a religion other than Islam (submission to God), never will it be accepted of him; and in the hereafter he will be in the ranks of those who have lost (all spiritual good)
>
> (Surah 3:85)

The Qur'an teaches that all people are created by Allah and are therefore equal:

> And among His signs is the creation of the heavens and the earth, and the variations in your languages and your colours.
>
> (Surah 30:21)

> O mankind! We created you from a single (pair) of a male and a female, and made you into nations and tribes, that ye may know each other (not that ye may despise each other). Verily the most honoured of you in the sight of God is (he who is) the most Righteous of you. And God has full knowledge and is well acquainted (with all things).
>
> (Surah 49:13)

Prejudice and discrimination

Muslims are not a particular racial group: followers of Islam can be found all over the world and so there can never be any excuse for racism or prejudice.

In his last sermon Prophet Muhammad said:

> All mankind is descended from Adam and Eve, an Arab is not better than a non-Arab and a non-Arab is not better than an Arab; a white person is not better than a black person, nor is a black person better than a white person expect by piety and good actions. Learn that every Muslim is the brother or every other Muslim and that Muslims form one brotherhood.

Islam teaches that men and women are equal and that Allah will judge them equally according to the way in which they have lived.

To help men value women for who they are, rather than for their bodies, Muslim women wear garments that leave only the hands and face exposed.

> O Prophet! Tell thy wives and daughters, and the believing women, that they should cast their outer garments over their persons (when abroad): that is most convenient, that they should be known (as such) and not molested.
>
> (Surah 33:59)

Many non-Muslim Westerners cannot understand Islamic teaching about women and feel that the need for women to be covered up in public and the way in which they are brought up is wrong. According to Islam, the rights and responsibilities of a woman are equal to those of a man, but they are not identical. Therefore, they should be complementary to each other rather than competitive.

> And women shall have rights similar to the rights against them, according to what is equitable; but men have a degree (of advantage) over them.
>
> (Surah 2:228)

Men are the protectors and maintainers of women, because God has given the one more (strength) than the other, and because they support them from their means.

(Surah 4:34)

In Islam, this difference is seen as both natural and desirable. Men must support the family while women bear and rear children. Women have the right to study, refuse a marriage, to divorce, to inherit, to keep their own names, to own property, to take part in politics, and to conduct business, whether they are married or unmarried.

Prophet Muhammad stressed the respect which should be shown to women:

Paradise lies at the feet of your mother.

(Sunan An-Nasa'i)

War and peace

The Arabic word **jihad** is often wrongly translated as 'Holy War'. Jihad means 'to struggle in the way of Allah'. It is the personal effort made by every Muslim to devote his or her life to carrying out Allah's will and also means the fight against evil.

The Prophet was asked about people fighting because they are brave, or in honour of a certain loyalty, or to show off: which of them fights for the cause of Allah? He replied, 'The person who struggles so that Allah's word is supreme is the one serving Allah's cause.'

(Hadith)

The name for a Holy War is **Harb al-Muqadis**. Self-defence is a just cause for war but Muslims are forbidden from being the first to attack.

Fight in the cause of God Those who fight you, But do not transgress limits; For God loveth not transgressors.

(Surah 2:190)

Muslims see jihad as a way to peace. The aim is to create a society where they can worship Allah in peace, without other beliefs or politics being forced upon them. According to the Qur'an and the sayings of the Prophet (contained in the Hadith), Muslims are forbidden from starting a war. If the enemy offers peace, then Muslims, too, must put down their weapons. In countries where Islam governs politics as well as religion, living in a democracy is seen as something which people should fight for if necessary.

Peace in Islam does not mean accepting a situation if it is unjust, but enemies and oppressors must be fought without hatred or vengeance, and once the battle is over, peace must be restored and differences reconciled.

Hate your enemy mildly; he may become your friend one day.

(Hadith)

A man asked Prophet Muhammad (pbuh), 'O Messenger of Allah! Who deserves the best care from me?' The Prophet said, 'Your mother.' The man asked, 'Who then?' The Prophet said, 'Your mother.' The man asked yet again, 'Who then?' Prophet Muhammad (pbuh) said, 'Your mother.' The man asked once more, 'Who then?' The Prophet then said, 'Your father.'
(Sahih Al-Bukhari)

A food distribution centre, Bangladesh

Summary

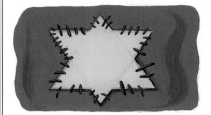

So, how should we respond when something really 'isn't fair'? It seems that each of these religions believes that we should take some action to try to make life fairer.

Whatever we do, it is likely to be a long time before we can really say that everyone is treated fairly and that all people are living in peace. Nevertheless, this is a goal which each of these religions believes that we should try to reach so that everyone can have a better, happier and fairer life.

A gay rally, New Orleans.

1 What do you understand by:

   prejudice

   discrimination

   fair, reasonable and equitable

   racism

   sexism

   pacifism?

2 Consider whether there really are occasions when we should take the life of another human being.

3 How far is it fair to describe Dietrich Bonhoeffer as a pacifist?

4 Do you think that it is possible for a member of one of these religions to be a pacifist and a true believer?

5 Do you think these religions should adapt to give women a greater role or should women be content with their responsibilities for their husband and the family?

6 Consider whether religious people should involve themselves in political questions such as issues of war and racism.

7 How far do you think members of different religions should try to overcome their differences and work together for the good of everyone? Is this a realistic aim?

7 Is anything really sacred?

People often say: 'Is nothing sacred?' when they hear about something taking place which they object to.

Most religious people believe that life is a gift from their God or Gods, even though they know that they were created by the actions of human beings. Because of this, they often react quite strongly when it appears that humans are interfering with life.

The four issues which we will consider here are contraception, abortion, euthanasia and drugs. Each of these is involved with the prevention, possible harming, or ending of life by human hands.

A popular saying goes: 'The Lord gives and the Lord takes away'. This is meant to imply that only God can influence life.

Contraception is the voluntary prevention of conception, 'birth control'. Contraception may be used for a number of reasons:

- for cases in which pregnancy and therefore childbirth might harm the mental or physical condition of the mother
- to limit the number of children which people have in order to maintain or improve their living standards
- by people who have sexual relationships with each other but who do not want to have children.

Abortion is the expulsion of a foetus from the uterus before it has reached the stage of viability (usually about the 20th week of gestation). Abortions are usually performed for one of four reasons:

- to preserve the physical or mental well-being of the mother
- to prevent a pregnancy when a woman is raped
- to prevent a child being born mentally or physically damaged.

Euthanasia is sometimes called 'mercy killing'. Euthanasia is the act of painlessly putting someone to death. There are three types of voluntary euthanasia:

- people may decide to take their own life or refuse medical treatment which would keep them alive
- a doctor may agree not to forcibly keep someone alive when they are in great pain and have expressed a wish not to be kept alive
- they may persuade someone else to help them die but this counts as murder.

Drugs: here we are considering drugs which are not prescribed by a doctor, sometimes known as 'leisure' or 'illegal' drugs. These include drugs such as LSD and Ecstasy, as well as more common 'social' drugs like alcohol and tobacco.

A leaflet from Life, a pro-life organisation.

Life
CARES FOR YOU

FREE PREGNANCY TESTING
ACCOMMODATION AND ADVICE ON HOUSING
COUNSELLING – PREGNANCY AND POST ABORTION
ADVICE AND PRACTICAL FOLLOW-UP CARE

REGISTERED CHARITY NO. 274144

A family of Hasidic Jews, Jerusalem.

According to the Jewish scriptures God created the world and, at the same time, he created men and women.

Then God said, 'Let us make man in our image, in our likeness, and let them rule over the fish of the sea and the birds of the air, over the livestock, over all the earth, and over all the creatures that move along the ground.' So God created man in his own image, in the image of God he created him; male and female he created them.

God blessed them and said to them, 'Be fruitful and increase in number; fill the earth and subdue it. Rule over the fish of the sea and the birds of the air and over every living creature that moves on the ground.'

(Genesis 1:26–28)

Jews believe that, since God created human beings, only he is in charge of when they live and when they die.

Sexual relationships within a marriage are a very important part of Judaism. They are seen as a husband's duty and a woman's right, so the questions of contraception and abortion are very important.

Contraception

The passage from Genesis above says that people should, 'Be fruitful and increase in number; fill the earth…' This is one of the reasons that Judaism is opposed to the use of birth control. This idea is repeated much later by Isaiah when he says:

he who fashioned and made the earth… he did not create it to be empty, but formed it to be inhabited

(Isaiah 45:18)

However, any restriction on the use of contraceptives can be lifted if a married woman would be placed at risk, either physically or psychologically, by becoming pregnant.

Contraception is not allowed when people are not married or simply feel that they do not want a child: this is viewed as interfering with God's plan. When contraceptives are used, they are usually taken by the woman so that sexual intercourse is still as natural as possible. Condoms are thought to interfere with the physical relationship between couples:

For this reason a man will leave his father and mother and be united to his wife, and they will become one flesh.

(Genesis 2:24)

The use of condoms is now recommended to help prevent the spread of the HIV virus, but they are not generally permitted by Jewish teaching. In the same way, neither sterilisation or vasectomy are permitted, as they mutilate the body.

Abortion

Judaism considers that abortion is worse than contraception because not only does it interfere with God's plan, but it also destroys what has the potential to become a human being.

Many Jews now accept that there are some instances when abortion is permissible. The life and well-being of the mother is the most important issue and abortion is acceptable if the mother is at risk either physically or mentally. The mother must be the person who decides in these circumstances. Abortion would never be approved simply for the sake of convenience and the later in the pregnancy the mother is, the more difficult it becomes for Judaism to sanction it.

Euthanasia

In general terms Judaism does not approve of euthanasia because only God can decide when a person should die. However the teaching of Rabbi Moses Isserles is sometimes used to argue that life-support machines should be turned off if there is no hope of the patient's recovery:

If there is anything which causes a hindrance to the departure of the soul... then it is permissible to remove it.

Drugs

Alcohol, like wine, is an important part of most Jewish festivals and ceremonies including marriage and the service of kiddush on the Sabbath. A blessing is said when wine is drunk: 'Blessed are you, Lord our God, King of the Universe, who creates the fruit of the vine.'

Smoking is not forbidden in Judaism, although people are expected to be conscious of their health. However, all sorts of mind-altering drugs, taken for pleasure, are forbidden as damaging God's Creation.

According to the Jewish scriptures, the life of a human being is more important than the life of the unborn child. This is shown in this passage from Exodus:

If men who are fighting hit a pregnant woman and she gives birth prematurely but there is no serious injury, the offender must be fined whatever the woman's husband demands and the court allows. But if there is serious injury, you are to take life for life...

(Exodus 21:22-23)

A patient in intensive care.

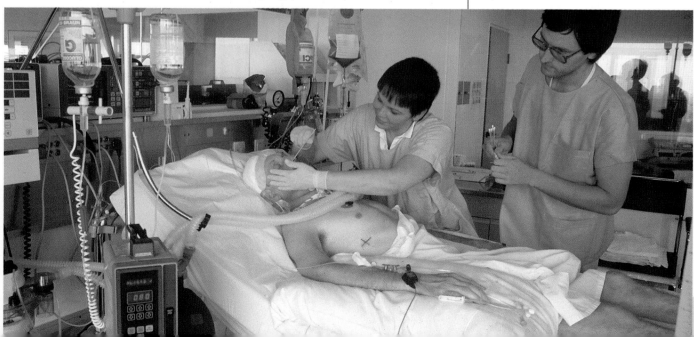

Christianity regards life as sacred and as a gift from God.

Then God said, 'Let us make man in our image, in our likeness, and let them rule over the fish of the sea and the birds of the air, over the livestock, over all the earth, and over all the creatures that move along the ground.' So God created man in his own image, in the image of God he created him; male and female he created them.

(Genesis 1:26–27)

Contraception

The Roman Catholic Church bases much of its teaching on Natural Law (what is in keeping with human nature). Because it is natural that conception may follow from intercourse, the Catholic Church does not approve of any form of contraception which would prevent this from taking place. Therefore the only form of contraception which is permitted is the rhythm method which, it is said, makes use of the body's natural cycle.

The Church argues that humans have an obligation from God to 'Be fruitful and increase in number' and that this is in accordance with Natural Law.

The Methodist Church welcomes contraception as a means of spacing a family and providing fulfilment in marriage. The Anglican Church also says that the responsibility for deciding upon the number and frequency of children was given by God to the parents' conscience 'in such ways as are acceptable to man and wife' (Lambeth Conference).

Abortion

Abortion is a complex issue in Christianity and has caused many problems and debates within the Churches. None of the Christian Churches feel that abortion should be encouraged or used in any but the most serious circumstances.

The Roman Catholic Church is very strongly opposed to abortion in all cases. The only exception is in the instance of 'double effect' when a necessary operation to the mother may require a pregnancy to be terminated. It is argued that the foetus is a living person from the moment of conception, this can be known as:

- **ensoulment:** Thomas Aquinas argued that the male foetus becomes a human being 40 days after conception and the female, 90 days after conception
- **quickening:** the time when the baby starts to move in the womb

Anti-abortion protesters, Chicago, USA.

Anti-abortionists argue from Natural Law and also from the Bible:

'For you created my inmost being; you knit me together in my mother's womb.'

(Psalm 139:13)

'Before I formed you in the womb I knew you, before you were born I set you apart'

(Jeremiah 1:5)

This is often supported by the following experience of John the Baptist's mother, Elizabeth which appears in the Bible:

When Elizabeth heard Mary's greeting, the baby leaped in her womb, and Elizabeth was filled with the Holy Spirit.

(Luke 1:41)

The Didache, one of the earliest Christian documents, said:

You shall not kill by abortion the fruit of the womb.

In 1993 the General Synod of the Church of England said that far too many abortions were being carried out. It encouraged people to realise just how serious a moral decision they were making and that abortion should not be seen as an ultimate form of contraception. However, it still left the issue up to the consciences of the people concerned.

Perhaps the most open view of abortion comes from the Religious Society of Friends (Quakers). Although abortion can be seen as going against their commitment to pacifism and non-violence, they would not value the life of an unborn child above that of the woman concerned.

Euthanasia

Euthanasia, whether voluntary or involuntary, is condemned by many Christians as murder and as breaking the Sixth Commandment:

You shall not murder.

(Exodus 20:13)

The Roman Catholic Church argues that any action which is intended to cause death is 'a grave violation of the law of God' (Evangelium Vitae). This covers the giving of an overdose of painkillers as well as withholding treatment from a person if it is known that they will then die. Large doses of painkillers which are required to ease suffering but which, by the law of 'double effect', will probably ultimately cause death are permitted. In the same way any 'extraordinary treatment' to keep a person alive when they are in a Persistent Vegetative State is not required.

In 1992, the Church of England recognised that although 'the deliberate taking of human life is prohibited except in self-defence or the legitimate defence of others' there were very strong arguments that people should not be kept alive at all costs when they were suffering intolerable pain.

Similar distinctions are made by most of the other Christian Churches, they fear that a change in the law to legalise euthanasia would be abused and elderly people might be put under pressure to accept euthanasia. Also they encourage support of the Hospice Movement which is committed to helping the elderly and terminally ill die with comfort and dignity.

Dr Jack Kevorkian known as 'Doctor Death' was found not guilty of helping terminally ill patients to commit suicide.

Christians believe that life is sacred:

'your body is a temple of the Holy Spirit'
(1 Corinthians 6:19)

They do not approve of the taking of so-called 'leisure drugs'. Alcohol is permitted by most Christians and, of course, is normally used for the celebration of the Eucharist.

after supper he took the cup, saying, 'This cup is the new covenant in my blood; do this, whenever you drink it, in remembrance of me.'
(1 Corinthians 11:24)

A Muslim family in Azerbaijan.

Islam teaches that Allah created the world and everything in it.

To God belongs the dominion of the heavens and the earth. He creates what He wills (and plans).

(Surah 42:49)

Life is therefore a special gift.

Contraception

For Muslims, the birth of a child is not an 'accident' and does not happen by mistake, it is a gift of life from Allah.

He bestows (children) male or female according to His will (and plan). Or He bestows both males and females, and He leaves barren whom He will.

(Surah 42:49-50)

Because of this view, contraception is not welcomed in Islam. However, in 1971, the Conference on Islam and Family Planning agreed that safe and legal contraception was permitted under certain circumstances:
- if there is a threat to the mother's health
- if contraception can help a woman who already has children
- where there is a chance of the child being born with mental or physical deformities
- where the family does not have the money to raise a child

Generally, Muslims prefer the use of the rhythm method of contraception: intercourse only takes place at the time of the month when the woman is known to be least fertile. Other artificial methods of contraception, such as condoms or the Pill, are used in preference to permanent sterilisation or vasectomy.

Abortion

Although contraception is permitted in some circumstances, generally Islam will not permit abortion. It is thought of as a crime against a living human being and so, if an abortion is carried out, blood money can be payable for the loss of life.

However, abortion is allowed if a doctor is convinced that continuation of the pregnancy will result in the mother's death. The later in the pregnancy that an abortion takes place, the more human the foetus, and so the greater the crime. Some Muslims believe that for the first four months of pregnancy the mother's rights are greater than those of the child. After this time, they have equal rights.

Before the time of Prophet Muhammad unwanted baby girls were often buried alive in Arabia. The Qur'an has very strict rules against this which are now also applied to abortion:

O ye who believe! seek help with patient perseverance and prayer: for God is with those who patiently persevere...Be sure we shall test you with something of fear and hunger, some loss in goods or lives or the fruits (of your toil), but give glad tidings to those who patiently persevere, – who say, when afflicted with calamity: 'To God we belong, and to Him is our return'.

(Surah 2:153-156)

Kill not your children for fear of want: We shall provide sustenance for them as well as for you. Verily the killing of them is a great sin.

(Surah 17:31)

For what crime was she killed?

(Surah 81:9)

If a pregnant woman is sentenced to death for a crime, she cannot be executed until after the baby is born.

Euthanasia

Muslims are opposed to euthanasia as they are also opposed to suicide.
Because every soul is created by Allah, life is sacred. It is forbidden for a person to kill him or herself.

Nor kill (or destroy) yourselves: for verily God hath been to you Most Merciful!

(Surah 4:29)

Whatever happens to a person, no matter how painful, it is never a good enough reason to end life, whether by suicide or euthanasia.

When their Term expires, they would not be able to delay (the punishment) for a single hour, just as they would not be able to anticipate it (for a single hour).

(Surah 16:61)

Nor can a soul die, except by God's leave, the term being fixed as by writing.

(Surah 3:145)

Drugs

Islam is opposed to the use of any drugs except those which are medically prescribed.

Prophet Muhammad (pbuh) said, 'Every intoxicant is khamr (alcohol) and all khamr is haram (unlawful or not permitted)'.

This was stated in the Qur'an:

O ye who believe! Intoxicants… are an abomination, – of Satan's handiwork: eschew such (abomination) that ye may prosper. Satan's plan is (but) to excite enmity and hatred between you, with intoxicants and gambling, and hinder you from the remembrance of God, and from prayer.

(Surah 50:93-94)

It was thought that all drugs helped people to escape from real life and so they would not serve Allah well.
Tobacco is not specifically mentioned as being **haram**, but some Muslims say it is **makruh** (strongly disliked).

The Prophet Muhammad said that anyone who killed themselves would go to hell:

Anyone who throws themselves down from a rock and commits suicide will be throwing themselves into Hell. A person who drinks poison and kills themselves will drink it for ever in Hell. A person who stabs themselves will stab themselves for ever in Hell.

(Hadith)

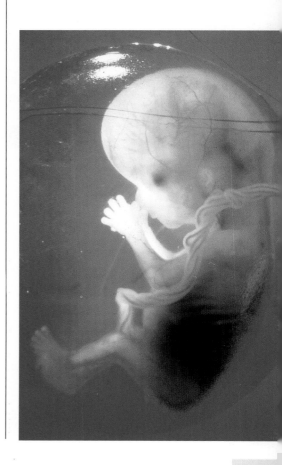

Summary

Despite the differences between them, these three religions have very similar views on most of these issues. We might conclude that '*Life really is sacred*' and that followers of these faiths believe that they are given life by God and must do all they can to respect and preserve it. All four of these issues: contraception, abortion, euthanasia and drugs will affect most of us, or people we know, at some time in our lives. None of them are matters which can be easily dismissed.

1 What do you understand by:

contraception

abortion

euthanasia

prescribed and 'leisure drugs'

a Hospice

Persistent Vegetative State?

2 Consider whether there is an argument that life is sacred and that we cannot do just what we want with it.

3 Do you think that people should make up their own minds about contraception or should they be mainly guided by religious teachings?

4 What factors should be taken into account when someone is thinking about having an abortion?

5 Explain why some people disagree with 'a woman's right to choose'.

6 Consider the arguments for and against Hospice care and euthanasia.

7 'In the 21st century people are well educated enough to make up their own minds about these issues, they do not need religions to tell them what to do.' Explain how far you would agree or disagree with this statement.

8 A question of dying

So, what does happen when we die? What comes next? These are some of the most important questions that people ever ask themselves. As far as we know animals do not worry about what is going to happen next. They live day by day and their concerns are simply feeding and breeding.

It is likely that since the first person died, humans have been worrying about what happens when they die. Many people believe that when they die that will be the end. They will not be conscious any more and so they will not know what is happening to them. Others think that they will continue to live on as ghosts. Some people think that after death they will be rewarded, or punished, by God for the way in which they have lived their lives. This might be in some sort of heaven or hell.

Death is the one certain thing about our lives. We cannot be sure whether we will be rich or successful. We cannot know if we will fall in love. We do know, however, that eventually we will stop breathing and we will die.

Death affects everyone during their lives. In an average year approximately 659,000 people die in Britain. For almost every one of these deaths, some people will be mourning and grieving because they have lost a relative or a friend.

Followers of Hinduism and Buddhism believe that, after they have died, they may be reborn many times. If you were a particularly bad person, for example, you might come back as an animal or even as an insect. You would have to die and be reborn many times before you have the opportunity of being a human being again. On the other hand, you might have lived such a good life that you are freed from this cycle of birth and rebirth and your soul is finally free to go to the afterlife.

A continuing series of lives is usually called **reincarnation**. You may have heard stories of people who claim to remember their previous lives and who, perhaps under hypnosis, can recall events of these earlier times. Although a lot of research has been carried out into these claims, no one so far has been able to prove that such a reincarnation has happened. Followers of Hinduism and Buddhism do not claim to be able to remember previous existences in this way.

The religions that we are studying in this book say that people only live once. What they believe will happen to them when they die, however, can be quite different.

Fans at the grave of Jim Morrison (1943–71), American singer and songwriter, in Paris.

The biblical book Maccabees describes the persecution which the Jews suffered from the Greeks. In one part, a man is being put to death because he refuses to say that he does not believe in God. He says that he would rather die knowing that he will eventually live with God. He also says that that the person who puts him to death will not have this resurrection:

> When he was near death, he said, 'One cannot but choose to die at the hands of mortals and to cherish the hope God gives of being raised again by him. But for you there will be no resurrection to life!'
>
> (2 Maccabees 7:14)

At the time when most of the Jewish scriptures were written, Jews believed that after death everyone went to **Sheol**. They believed that this was a dark, damp place where people's souls went after death and where they stayed for eternity. Jews believed that Adam and Eve would have lived forever in the Garden of Eden but, because they disobeyed God, they became mortal. From that time, everyone has grown old and eventually died.

For a long time in their early history Jews believed that they would be punished for anything bad which their parents or grandparents had done. This is shown in the following passage from the Book of Lamentations:

> *Our fathers sinned and are no more, and we bear their punishment.*
>
> (Lamentations 5:7)

Later, in this early period, they came to believe that it was how well they had lived their own lives which was important.

> *The word of the Lord came to me: 'What do you people mean by quoting this proverb about the land of Israel: "The fathers eat sour grapes, and the children's teeth are set on edge?" As surely as I live,' declares the Sovereign Lord, 'you will no longer quote this proverb in Israel. For every living soul belongs to me, the father as well as the son—both alike belong to me. The soul who sins is the one who will die.'*
>
> (Ezekiel 18:1–4)

Towards the end of the biblical period, Jews came to the idea that there might be some kind of eternal life with God after death. They also believed, however, that eventually God would judge people and that those who had not led good lives would go to hell.

The funeral of Yitzhak Rabin (1922–95), Prime Minister of Israel, assassinated by an Israeli right-wing activist.

When people die

Before they die, Jews try to say the Shema, a prayer showing belief in one God:

Hear, O Israel: Hashem is our God, Hashem, the One and Only. You shall love HASHEM, your God, with all your heart, with all your soul and with all your resources. Let these matters, which I command you today, be upon your heart. Teach them thoroughly to your children and speak of them while you sit in your home, while you walk on the way, when you retire and when you arise. Bind them as a sign upon your arm and let them be tefillin between your eyes. And write them on the doorposts of your house and upon your gates.

In Judaism, people do not mourn for long periods of time. The body is buried within twenty-four hours of death. It is washed and dried and dressed in **tachrichim** (a simple white shroud), and, if a man, wrapped in a **tallit** (prayer shawl). The fringes are cut from the prayer shawl to show that the man is now freed from the religious laws that bound him on earth. The body is placed in a plain wooden coffin and a simple service takes place at the graveside – everyone is equal in death.

Graves in a Jewish cemetery.

When someone dies, Jews say the Kaddish:

May His great Name grow exalted and sanctified in the world that He created as He willed. May He give reign to His kingship in your lifetime and in your days, and in the lifetimes of the entire Family of Israel, swiftly and soon. May His great Name be blessed forever and ever. Blessed, praised, glorified, exalted, extolled, mighty, upraised, and lauded be the Name of the Holy One, Blessed is He beyond any blessing and song, praise and consolation that are uttered in the world. May there be abundant peace from Heaven, and life, upon us and upon all Israel. He Who makes peace in His heights, may He may peace upon us, and upon all Israel.

According to Christianity, when Jesus died at his crucifixion and was resurrected three days later, he overcame the power of death and people were forgiven their sins.

Christians believe that Adam and Eve brought 'original sin' on to humanity when they disobeyed God in the Garden of Eden. Jesus' death cleaned people of this 'original sin'. It meant that they were freed of the punishment of original sin and, from that time, have the opportunity to go to heaven.

Jesus said, 'I am the resurrection and the life. He who believes in me will live, even though he dies; and whoever lives and believes in me will never die.'

(John 11:25–26)

Christianity teaches that one day Jesus will come back to the earth. This second coming of Christ is called the **parousia**. At the parousia, God will judge everyone. Those who have lived very bad lives will go to hell, but those who have followed Christian teachings and believe in Jesus will go to heaven.

Listen, I tell you a mystery: We will not all sleep, but we will all be changed – in a flash, in the twinkling of an eye, at the last trumpet. For the trumpet will sound, the dead will be raised imperishable, and we will be changed.

(1 Corinthians 15:51–52)

Roman Catholics believe in heaven and hell, but they also believe that there is an intermediate place known as **purgatory**. This is a place where Christians go who still need to be cleansed of some of the sins they have committed on earth. In purgatory, they are punished for a period of time before they are allowed to go to heaven.

Traditionally, Christians describe heaven as a beautiful garden paradise where they will live with God. Hell, on the other hand, is an eternal bonfire where people will suffer horrible torments from the devil. Nowadays, however, most people would understand these ideas as states of happiness or unhappiness. In heaven you will be with God for ever, while in hell you will never see God or know God's love again.

The Book of Revelation contains a description of what will happen on the Day of Judgement:

Then I saw a new heaven and a new earth, for the first heaven and the first earth had passed away, and there was no longer any sea. I saw the Holy City, the new Jerusalem, coming down out of heaven from God, prepared as a bride beautifully dressed for her husband. And I heard a loud voice from the throne saying, 'Now the dwelling of God is with men, and he will live with them. They will be his people, and God himself will be with them and be their God. He will wipe every tear from their eyes. There will be no more death or mourning or crying or pain, for the old order of things has passed away.'

(Revelation 21:1–7)

When people die

When a person is known to be dying, a minister or priest may visit them to say prayers or to read from the Bible. Some people will wish to confess their sins to a priest before death, but others may feel that this is a private matter between themselves and God. Roman Catholics receive the **Last Rites** from a priest. The priest will anoint them with holy oil as a preparation for death.

The Triumph of Death, *Breughel, Pieter the Elder (c. 1515–69)*

After death, Christians are usually buried or cremated. A funeral service usually takes place in a church and may be followed by a burial in the graveyard of the church or in a public cemetery. Some Christians will have a Requiem Mass said at the funeral, this is a Eucharist where prayers are said for the dead person's soul.

People often decorate the church with white flowers and flowers are put on the coffin and at the graveside. These represent the new life which the person is entering. Candles are also lit to remind Christians that they are saved because of Jesus who is the 'Light of the World'.

Prayers are said around the grave, and as the coffin is lowered into the ground, the priest or minister will say: 'We commit this body to the ground, earth to earth, ashes to ashes, dust to dust'. Later, a gravestone will be erected at the site of the grave. This has details of the person's life and possibly a quotation from the Bible. Relatives of the deceased person may take flowers to place on the grave.

This poem is read every year at Remembrance Day services to recall those who died fighting for their country:

> They shall not grow old, as we that are left grow old:
> Age shall not weary them, nor the years condemn.
> At the going down of the sun and in the morning
> We will remember them
>
> (Laurence Binyon)

The poem stresses the Christian belief that death is not something which people should be afraid of. Instead, they should look forward to a life in heaven when there will be no more suffering and where they will live happily with God for ever.

Many Christians, including Roman Catholics, do not approve of cremations because of the teachings of the Apostles' Creed which says:

> I believe in…
> the resurrection of the body,
> and the life everlasting.

This is very similar to the beliefs of the Ancient Greeks who thought that, in the afterlife, people continued to live in exactly the same physical condition in which they died.

However, in his first letter to the Christians at Corinth, Paul explained that in heaven people would have a perfect body which would be spiritual and not physical:

> The human body can grow old but in heaven it will not grow old, when people live on earth they sin and are weak but in heaven they will be strong and will not sin, on earth it is a physical body but in heaven it will be a spiritual body.
>
> (1 Corinthians 15:42–43)

The following Surah from the Qur'an teaches that people who have followed the words of Allah will live happily in a wonderful garden while people who have rejected these teachings will be punished:

> Then those who have believed And worked righteous deeds, shall be made happy in a Mead of Delight. And those who have rejected Faith and falsely denied Our Signs and the meeting of the Hereafter,–such shall be brought forth to punishment.
>
> (Surah 30:15-16)

Islam teaches that all people who believe in God will be judged at the last day. As well as Muslims, this includes Christians and Jews and an ancient race called the Sabians:

> Those who believe (in the Qur'an). Those who follow the Jewish (scriptures), and the Sabians and the Christians, –any who believe in God And the Last Day, And work righteousness,–on them shall be no fear, nor shall they grieve.
>
> (Surah 5:72)

Muslims believe that after death there will be a Day of Judgement. People who have not followed Allah's wishes will go to hell where they will be punished. Good people will go to a perfect world of rest and pleasure and be with Allah for **Akhirah** (life after death). Muslims do not believe that people have an immortal soul, but that when people die, they stay in the grave until the Day of Judgement. On this day, true followers of Allah will be 'reborn' in Paradise. Muslims believe that without a belief in life after death, life on earth would be meaningless.

Like Christians and Jews, Muslims believe that you only have one chance at life and you are judged on how you live it. When the judgement of Allah (God) finally comes he will already know everything and judgement will be fast and final:

> To God belongeth the mystery of the heavens and the earth and the decision of the Hour (of Judgment) is as the twinkling of an eye, or even quicker: For God hath power over all things.
>
> (Surah 16:77)

When people die

On their death bed, Muslims repeat the final words of the Prophet Muhammad 'Allah, help me through the hardship and agony of death'. When other Muslims hear of the death they say, 'To Allah we belong and to Allah we return', showing that they hope the person will be claimed by Allah to live in heaven.

Funerals take place within three days of death (if possible, within 24 hours). The body is washed and covered in a simple white cloth. If the laws of the country permit, no coffin is used. Muslims are buried facing Makkah. In the United Kingdom this sort of burial is not allowed and so Muslims have to use coffins.

Muslims believe in a complete physical resurrection of the body and so do not approve of cremation. The following verse points out that Allah will have no difficulty in putting these dead bodies back together, including their fingerprints:

> Does man think that We cannot assemble his bones? Nay, We are able to put together in perfect order the very tips of his fingers.
>
> (Surah 75:3-4)

A Muslim graveyard in Tunisia.

At the graveside Surah 1 of the Qu'ran, **al–Fatihah**, is recited. This is a very important statement of belief in Allah and his mercy. Muslims always say al-Fatihah when praying:

In the name of God, Most Gracious, Most Merciful. Praise be to God, the Cherisher and Sustainer of the Worlds; Most Gracious, Most Merciful; Master of the Day of Judgment. Thee do we worship, and Thine aid we seek. Show us the straight way, the way of those on whom Thou hast bestowed Thy Grace those whose (portion) is not wrath, and who go not astray.

(Surah 1)

As the coffin is lowered into the ground, the mourners say the following words. These words show their belief that Allah will take the dead to Paradise at the Day of Judgement:

From the (earth) did We create you, and into it shall We return you, and from it shall We bring you out once again.

(Surah 20:55)

It is traditional for the grave to be raised a little above the level of the ground to stop people walking or sitting on it, but elaborate monuments are forbidden.

Summary

Although followers of these three religions all believe in some sort of life after death, they have different beliefs about what exactly will happen to them when they die. One of the main concerns of religious people is how they will be judged and treated for the life that they have led on earth. Some people believe that if they confess their sins or repent before they die, they will receive better treatment from God.

People have different beliefs about heaven and hell. In the past, many people thought that heaven and hell were simply physical places: heaven above and hell below. These days, however, we have a greater understanding of the earth and the universe, and people have come to rather different conclusions.

Some people now say that heaven and hell are types of existence and that it is only people's souls which are there, not their bodies. Others say that heaven and hell are where we live now and that we create them for ourselves.

What is certain about all of these beliefs is that we cannot really know what will happen after death until we have died. People may be certain in their faith and believe strongly that something will happen to them but, at the moment, we have no scientific proof about any other existence after death. It is a matter of faith and belief not of scientifically provable fact.

1 What do you understand by:

death

heaven

hell

purgatory

reincarnation

resurrection?

2 Try to explain how you think people may feel when someone close to them dies.

3 Explain how the way in which a funeral takes place in each of the three religions may be designed to help the relatives and friends of the person who has died.

4 Explain what you think may happen to you when you die.

5 Consider how important living a 'good' life is for what might happen to people when they die. What do you think a 'good' life is?

6 Do you think that people should be judged on the way in which they have lived their own lives or on the way in which their family, or the people in their country, or the people who follow their religion behave?

9 Are love and sex the same thing?

Love: warm affection or attachment to a person. *Sex:* meaning sexual intercourse, often used in the phrase 'to have sex (with)'.

Most people would probably say that they know what human love is, even if they have only experienced love for a parent, or a brother or sister. They may say that friendship is a way of showing human love, too. Also, everyone would probably say that they knew what sexual activity is – they may not have experienced it with anyone, but they still know what is involved.

Some people might say that love and sex are really the same thing, or they may behave as though they are the same thing. This is very obvious when people say that they 'made love'. In fact, the people concerned may not love one another at all, they have actually had sexual intercourse with each other.

This is an area of discussion where people like to laugh and make smutty jokes, but in fact, it is an issue of very real and serious concern within religious teaching.

One of the questions which we are trying to answer, or at least discuss, is whether these are really two different words for the same thing, or if there is a very real and important difference between them. The religions that we are studying do see a difference, but the activities of many people of all ages throughout the world, often seem to suggest the opposite.

The other question to be discussed in this chapter is: *why* do religions treat the two as separate?

The marriage service of the Church of England says that one of the purposes of marriage is as:

'a remedy against sin, and to avoid fornication; that such persons as have not the gift of continency might marry'

(The Book of Common Prayer)

The Church believes that it is a sin for people to have sexual relations with each other unless they are married. It also suggests that marriage is only required when people are not able to manage to live celibate lives. The teaching seems to imply that sex is wrong, but that marriage somehow makes it less of a sin.

We need to ask why some religions have this view about sexual intercourse, after all, it is the way in which people have children and, like other animals, people were clearly designed to produce new life.

Jewish moral behaviour is laid down by **mitzvot** (rules) found in the Torah and the Talmud (Oral Torah). Judaism has a very natural and realistic view of sexuality and sexuality plays a very important part in human relationships. Judaism recognises the strength of sexual desire but also sees that this must be carefully controlled. It may only be expressed within a marriage.

Unlike Christianity, the idea of religious celibacy does not exist within Judaism. It is believed that God wished men and women to serve him by living together and producing families like the leaders in the Bible such as Abraham, Jacob and Moses. Therefore it would be 'abnormal' for people to live celibate lives like monks or nuns.

The family is a very important part of Judaism. When Abraham was a very old man, God promised that he would have many descendants:

> *'Look up at the heavens and count the stars – if indeed you can count them… So shall your offspring be.'*
>
> (Genesis 15:5)

Many Jews still have very large families and the family is the centre of all Jewish life and worship.

Jewish marriages are very important family occasions. They need not take place in a synagogue, but the **huppah** (marriage canopy) must be held over the bride and groom to represent the home which they will make together. Also, the groom signs a **Ketubah** (marriage contract) which states the promises and financial obligations which he is making to his wife.

A Jewish couple under a huppah.

Judaism does not believe that procreation is the only purpose for sex. It says that it is a physical way in which two married people can show their love for one another, even when they are too old to have children.

Adultery is forbidden by the Seventh Commandment and this law is strictly observed. Also, although some of the Jewish leaders found in the Bible had several wives, Jews today may only be married to one person.

Judaism has strict rules concerning the relationships between husband and wife. A married couple is considered to be a complete organism, but men and women on their own are incomplete, lacking the qualities of each other. Marriage sanctifies the relationship:

> *The mating of animals is a temporary and purely physical act. Through the sanctification of marriage, a husband and wife become the closest of relatives.*
>
> (Maimonides)

Within marriage, sex is 'controlled' or regulated by the laws of **niddah** (sexual purity). During a woman's monthly menstrual period she is not allowed to have sex with her husband. This then continues for a further week. After this time she goes to a ritual bath called a **mikveh** where she 'cleans' herself. After this she and her husband can resume normal sexual relations until her next period. This is mentioned in the Torah and the Talmud:

> *Do not come near a woman during her period of uncleanness.*
>
> (Leviticus 18:19)

> *A wife returning from the mikveh is as fresh to her husband as on their wedding day.*
>
> (Talmud)

Although the rules of niddah are observed by most Orthodox Jews, most Progressive Jews feel that they are now out of date.

Homosexuality is forbidden in Judaism. Male homosexuality is clearly wrong according to the Torah:

> *Do not lie with a male as one lies with a woman; it is an abhorrence.*
>
> (Leviticus 18:22)

Female homosexuality is not mentioned in the Torah but it is forbidden in the Talmud. Orthodox Jews adhere strictly to these rules. It is believed that homosexuality is a condition which is learned or brought about by circumstances and that people can be helped out of it.

Because Jewish teaching is concerned with the family and children, masturbation is also forbidden, although some people doubt whether this interpretation of the Bible is correct. Masturbation is known as the 'Sin of Onan' after a character in the book of Genesis who was killed, by God, when he 'spilled his semen on the ground'.

day, and hallowed it.
12 ¶ Honour thy father and thy mother: that thy days may be long upon the land which the LORD thy God giveth thee.
13 Thou shalt not kill.
14 Thou shalt not commit adultery.
15 Thou shalt not steal.
16 Thou shalt not bear false witness against thy neighbour.
17 Thou shalt not covet thy neighbour's house, thou shalt not covet thy

73

A wedding in an Anglican church.

A Christian nun praying.

What does Christianity say about love and sex?

First of all, the Christian Church takes the teaching of the Ten Commandments very seriously. The Seventh Commandment – *You shall not commit adultery* – is often interpreted to mean that people must not have a sexual relationship with anyone to whom they are not married and not simply that married people must not 'sleep' with someone else.

Jesus went further and said:

> 'You have heard that it was said, "Do not commit adultery." But I tell you that anyone who looks at a woman lustfully has already committed adultery with her in his heart.'
>
> (Matthew 5:27–28)

It seems that Christians feel that sexual intercourse is always wrong unless it takes place within a marriage. They believe that God intended men and women to live together as married couples, but not to cohabit.

Paul said that the body really belonged to God and so must be cared for:

> Flee from sexual immorality. All other sins a man commits are outside his body, but he who sins sexually sins against his own body. Do you not know that your body is a temple of the Holy Spirit, who is in you, whom you have received from God?
>
> (1 Corinthians 6:18–19)

In fact, according to the same letter, Paul seemed to believe that people should really be **celibate** (someone who leads a single life, a confirmed bachelor or spinster; someone who has decided not to marry). He remained unmarried:

> Now for the matters you wrote about: It is good for a man not to marry. But since there is so much immorality, each man should have his own wife, and each woman her own husband. The husband should fulfil his marital duty to his wife, and likewise the wife to her husband. The wife's body does not belong to her alone but also to her husband. In the same way, the husband's body does not belong to him alone but also to his wife. Do not deprive each other except by mutual consent and for a time, so that you may devote yourselves to prayer. Then come together again so that Satan will not tempt you because of your lack of self-control. I say this as a concession, not as a command. I wish that all men were as I am. But each man has his own gift from God; one has this gift, another has that. Now to the unmarried and the widows I say: It is good for them to stay unmarried, as I am. But if they cannot control themselves, they should marry, for it is better to marry than to burn with passion.
>
> (1 Corinthians 7:8–9)

This passage implies that Christianity sees sex as a very strong and dangerous emotion from which people have to protect themselves.

The Roman Catholic Church has a very strict attitude towards masturbation which it believes is always wrong. In addition, Roman Catholic priests, monks and nuns are all required to take a vow of celibacy because it is believed that having a sexual partner will distract them from working for God. Some Christians feel that this is unhealthy and not normal: God created men and women and gave them the desire to have sexual relationships with each other, so why should he want people to deny themselves? On the other hand, many Christians regard this as a sacrifice which they are making as a demonstration of the love for God.

Christians are urged to love one another in a platonic (non-sexual) way to show that they are living according to God's love.

As well as the discussion about love and sex, another issue which has always been a very important part of Christian teaching is homosexuality.

A homosexual is a person who is emotionally and sexually attracted to members of the same sex. The opposite is a heterosexual who is attracted to members of the opposite sex. Many people say that heterosexuals are 'normal' while homosexuals are 'abnormal'. Female homosexuals are usually known as lesbians but both men and women often describe themselves as gay.

The Old Testament says that homosexuality is wrong and some people believe that this was the reason that God destroyed the cities of Sodom and Gomorrah in Genesis chapter 14.

For many years the Church has said that feelings of homosexuality are acceptable but that people must live celibate lives because it would be a sin for them to take part in any sexual activity. In recent years this has been challenged by many people and there has been some attempt to soften the official Church policy. However, although many of the clergy are willing to accept homosexuals and homosexual couples in their congregations, only the Religious Society of Friends (Quakers) fully accept homosexuals who are actively sexually. Even the Methodist Church which has always been very open to discussion about this 'does not consider that homosexual genital practice…is acceptable'.

Here then we have a very clear example of where love and sex are certainly not regarded as the same thing. Between one in twenty and one in ten people are homosexual so it seems that many Christians are not permitted to be fully part of the Christian Church.

Ideas of Christian love are given in the New Testament:

Dear friends, let us love one another, for love comes from God. Everyone who loves has been born of God and knows God. Whoever does not love does not know God, because God is love. This is how God showed his love among us: He sent his one and only Son into the world that we might live through him. This is love: not that we loved God, but that he loved us and sent his Son as an atoning sacrifice for our sins. Dear friends, since God so loved us, we also ought to love one another. No-one has ever seen God; but if we love one another, God lives in us and his love is made complete in us.
(1 John 4:7–12)

Paul is very certain on the question of homosexuality and says:

God gave them over to shameful lusts. Even their women exchanged natural relations for unnatural ones. In the same way the men also abandoned natural relations with women and were inflamed with lust for one another. Men committed indecent acts with other men, and received in themselves the due penalty for their perversion.
(Romans 1:26–27)

Do you not know that the wicked will not inherit the kingdom of God? Do not be deceived: Neither the sexually immoral nor idolaters nor adulterers nor male prostitutes nor homosexual offenders nor thieves nor the greedy nor drunkards nor slanderers nor swindlers will inherit the kingdom of God.
(1 Corinthians 6:9–10)

Islam is often thought of as having very strict attitudes towards sex and sexual relationships. It is clear from Muslim teaching that sexual relationships are only permitted within marriage:

> *When a husband and wife are intimate it is rewarded and is a blessing from Allah, in the same way they are punished if they have sex outside of the marriage.*
>
> (Hadith)

In the same way, men are forbidden to be alone with women except for their wives, in case they are tempted by them:

> *Let no man be in privacy with a woman who he is not married to, or Satan will be the third.*
>
> (Hadith)

It could be said that Islam has a very realistic attitude towards sex and realises that both men and women can be tempted to have sexual relationships outside of marriage. For this reason, Islam does not have the same strict rules about masturbation which are found in some other religions, although these rules only apply to men. Masturbation is permitted if a man fears that otherwise he may commit adultery or have sex outside of marriage or if, for some reason, he is unable to marry. However, Prophet Muhammad recommended frequent fasting in order to control sexual desire:

> *Young men, those of you who can support a wife should marry, for it keeps you from looking at women and preserves your chastity; but those who cannot should fast, for it is a means of cooling sexual passion.*
>
> (Hadith)

Some people might say that this is an unnatural approach to what is a very natural and common activity.

Islam recognises that sex is a gift from Allah but insists that it may only take place within a marriage. Marriage and the family are the basis of Islamic society:

> *It is He who has created man from water: then has He established relationships of lineage and marriage.*
>
> (Surah 25:54)

> *No institution in Islam finds more favour with God than marriage.*
>
> (Hadith)

Many Muslim marriages are arranged by families. Courtship or 'going out with each other' is not permitted and the couple who may be married are only allowed to meet each other when members of their families are present. Although marriages like this may be arranged by families, no one can ever be forced to marry someone in Islam. If someone is forced, the marriage is invalid.

Sexual activity of any kind outside of marriage is forbidden:

> Nor come night to adultery:
> For it is a shameful (deed) and an evil, opening the road (to other evils).
>
> (Surah 17:32)

and the punishment is severe:

> The woman and the man guilty of adultery or fornication, — flog each of them with a hundred stripes: let not compassion move you in their case, in a matter prescribed by God, if ye believe in God and the Last Day..
>
> (Surah 24:2)

Men are urged to be careful about who they marry:

A woman is taken in marriage for three reasons; for her beauty, for family connections or the lure of wealth. Choose the one with faith and you will have success.

(Hadith).

Polygamy (having more than one wife) is permitted by Islamic law, but is not allowed in Britain.

Marry women of your choice, two, or three, or four; but if ye fear that ye shall not be able to deal justly (with them), then only one.

(Surah 4:3)

Polyandry (women having more than one husband) is forbidden.

Another very important part of a Muslim marriage is the **mahr** (dowry). This is paid by the man to the woman and becomes her personal property which she can do with as she wishes. The mahr may be money or jewellery or perhaps a copy of the Qur'an. Islamic law states that both men and women are people in their own right and a wife has the right to own property and keep her earnings.

The great importance of the way in which a husband and wife live together is stressed in the Qur'an:

He has created for you mates from among yourselves, that ye may dwell in tranquillity with them, And He has put love and mercy between your (hearts).

(Surah 30:21)

Usually, within a Muslim marriage, the wife stays in the home while the husband goes out to work. There is no rule about this, however, and it simply follows from the 'normal' practice of society. Men are expected to help at home, however, because Prophet Muhammad is known to have helped his wives.

As in Judaism and Christianity, homosexuality is forbidden in Islam. In practice, it is often ignored, though some Islamic lawyers have argued that it should be punished with the death penalty because it is impure.

Out of all creation have you selected only males for yourselves, and do you leave aside your wives whom your Lord created for you?

(Surah 26:165–166)

If two men among you are guilty of lewdness, punish them both. If they repent and amend leave them alone.

(Surah 4:16)

Similar rules are applied to female homosexuals:

Three persons shall not enter Paradise – the one who is disobedient to parents, the pimp, and the woman who imitates men.

(Hadith)

A Muslim couple on their wedding day.

Summary

On the question of love and sex, the views of these three religions are very similar. Perhaps the principal reason for this is because each religion stresses the importance of the family as the 'natural' way for people to live. For each religion, it is intended that families should bring new members into the religion so more people can find God.

As we have seen, however, the teachings of these religions are often rather different from the way in which many people live their lives today. The question we might ask, therefore, is whether or not it is the religions that are right, or today's society.

The Destruction of Sodom and Gomorrah, *John Martin (1789–1854)*

1 What do you understand by:

marriage

adultery

celibacy

cohabitation

polygamy and polyandry

homosexuality?

2 Consider whether there is really a difference between love and sex and what that difference might be.

3 Do you think it is possible for a person to be a member of one of these religions and to cohabit?

4 How far would you agree with the teachings of these religions about homosexuality (male and female) and why?

5 Explain why religions have a very strict attitude towards adultery.

6 Consider whether it is right for religious people to decide to deny their sexual desires and choose a life of celibacy or whether this is 'unnatural'.

7 In today's society is it realistic for religions to put so much stress on the family?

10 Till death (or something else) us do part

'Till death us do part' is a familiar phrase to most people, whether they are Christians or not. It is part of the marriage service and is, perhaps, the strongest vow that two people make to one another. Despite this, the number of divorces in the United Kingdom is rising: in 1961 the total number of divorces was 27,000; in 1993 it was 180,000. The number of people getting married, however, has stayed roughly the same: from 1961 to 1991 the number of marriages fell from 350,000 to about 340,000.

Marriage and the family lie at the centre of the teachings of most religions. It seems, however, that more and more people are finding it difficult to be married to one person for the whole of their lives.

So perhaps we have to consider why people are finding marriage difficult, or are choosing to live with another person in a close relationship without any legal ties.

One of the reasons why more people divorce or choose to cohabit, may be the way in which the law has changed. In the United Kingdom, before 1857, a person could only remarry by an Act of Parliament. Absolute divorce in a court was not allowed until 1857 and, until 1936, was only allowed in cases of adultery. After 1936, cruelty and desertion were also allowed as reasons for granting a divorce. Finally, in the 1970s, the law allowed people to be divorced when it could be shown that a marriage had 'irretrievably broken down'.

Another issue which is often linked with both divorce and cohabitation, is the status of any children which are born. Children who are born outside of a legal marriage, whether the parents are living together or not, are technically called illegitimate. In 1988, however, the law changed and since then, the married status of the parents of a child has been considered irrelevant. This has, to a large extent, changed social views about illegitimacy, although there are still many people who believe that it is 'wrong' for a child to be born 'outside of marriage'.

An aspect of marriage which occurs in many religious marriages is the giving of a dowry, this is a gift (often of money) from one partner to the other. In addition, before many marriages today, people make a contract which says not only how they will treat each other in the marriage, but also what will happen should they divorce.

Arnolfini marriage, *Jan van Eyck (1390–1441)*

Sheva Berachos (The Seven Blessings)
Blessed are You, HASHEM, our God, King of the universe, Who has created everything for His glory.

Blessed are You, HASHEM, our God, King of the universe, Who fashioned the Man. Blessed are You, HASHEM, our God, King of The universe, Who fashioned the Man in His image, in the image of his likeness. And prepared for him – from himself – a building for eternity. Blessed are You, HASHEM, Who fashioned the Man.

Bring intense joy – and exultation to the barren one – through the in-gathering of her children amidst her in gladness. Blessed are You, HASHEM, Who gladdens Zion through her children.

Gladden the beloved companions as You gladdened Your creature in the Garden of Eden from aforetime. Blessed are You, HASHEM, Who gladdens groom and bride.

Blessed are You, HASHEM, our God, King of the universe, Who created joy and gladness, groom and bride, mirth, glad song, pleasure, delight, love, brotherhood, peace, and companionship. HASHEM, our God, let there soon be heard in the cities of Judah and the streets of Jerusalem the sound of joy and the sound of gladness, the voice of the groom and the voice of the bride, the sound of the grooms' jubilance from their canopies and of youths from their song-filled feasts. Blessed are You, Who gladdens the groom with the bride.

Blessed are You HASHEM, our God, King of the universe, Who creates the fruit of the vine.

Marriage and the family have always been at the very centre of Jewish life. Many of the ceremonies of Jewish worship take place within the home and so kiddushin (marriage) is seen as being of very great importance. The Talmud says that:

> A man without a woman is doomed to an existence without joy, without blessing, without experiencing life's true goodness, without Torah, without protection and without peace.

A Jewish wedding may take place in a synagogue or anywhere else, but it is important for the bride and groom to stand under a **huppah** (wedding canopy). The huppah represents their new home together.

A very important part of the wedding is the **Ketubah**. This is a marriage contract in which the groom makes promises about how he will look after his wife. It is often a very beautifully decorated document and may hang over the bed in the new couple's home.

In the past, many Jews had an arranged wedding in which the couple were introduced to one another by a **shadchan** (matchmaker).

The importance of marriage in Judaism can be seen in the first book of the Torah, Genesis:

> a man will leave his father and mother and be united to his wife, and they will become one flesh

(Genesis 2:24)

This is explained in the Midrash:

> God created the first human being half male, half female. He then separated the two parts to form a man and a woman

The teacher, Maimonides said:

> Through the sanctification of marriage, a husband and wife become the closest of relatives.

A Jewish wedding ceremony is very short. At the centre of the ceremony lies the vow made by the man to the woman as he gives her a ring:

> Behold, you are consecrated to me by means of this ring, according to the rituals of Moses and Israel.

After this the Sheva Berachos (Seven Blessings) are said over a glass of wine.

During the ceremony the groom smashes a glass under his foot. The reason for this ritual is unknown. Some people say that it shows that marriage can be fragile, others say that it represents the destruction of the Jerusalem Temple in 70CE and the sadness of much of Jewish history.

Although Jews believe that marriage is for life, they do accept that sometimes divorce is inevitable. In these circumstances a man must issue his wife with a **get**, this is a divorce document from a **Beth Din** (Rabbinical Court). The rule is found in the book of Deuteronomy:

> *If a man marries a woman who becomes displeasing to him because he finds something indecent about her… he writes her a certificate of divorce, gives it to her and sends her from his house.*

(Deuteronomy 24:1)

The divorce is not allowed to take place for three months, in order to ensure that the woman is not pregnant.

Without a get neither a man nor a woman can remarry. No one can be forced to issue a get and so, even if a husband has left his wife, he can still refuse to divorce her. The woman may obtain a civil divorce, but she is still married according to Jewish law. However, people would not respect a man who refused to give his wife a get in these circumstances. Many people see this practice as unfair and sexist, and Progressive Jews today may allow the woman to obtain a get.

One of the major problems for many Jews today is the number of people who 'marry out' of their religion. In the past, most Jewish communities lived close together, in areas which were known as ghettos. Here they mixed almost entirely with other Jews and so they married other Jews. Today, many young Jews live and work outside of these closely-knit communities and some have met and fallen in love with people who are not Jewish. Very Orthodox Jews do not permit such marriages. Sometimes the father of a young man or woman who intends to marry someone who is not Jewish, may disown their child and say the Kaddish (the prayer said at funerals). This shows that to them that child is dead.

> *Do not intermarry with them. Do not give your daughters to their sons or take their daughters for your sons, for they will turn your sons away from following me to serve other gods, and the Lord's anger will burn against you and will quickly destroy you.*

(Deuteronomy 7:3-4)

As an increasing number of people do marry non-Jews, the number of Jewish weddings and of people taking an active part in their religion is falling.

A Ketubah

Jesus attended a wedding at Cana in Galilee:

On the third day a wedding took place at Cana in Galilee. Jesus' mother was there, and Jesus and his disciples had also been invited to the wedding. When the wine was gone, Jesus' mother said to him, 'They have no more wine.' 'Dear woman, why do you involve me?' Jesus replied. 'My time has not yet come.'

His mother said to the servants, 'Do whatever he tells you.'

Nearby stood six stone water jars, the kind used by the Jews for ceremonial washing, each holding from twenty to thirty gallons.

Jesus said to the servants, 'Fill the jars with water'; so they filled them to the brim. Then he told them, 'Now draw some out and take it to the master of the banquet.'

They did so, and the master of the banquet tasted the water that had been turned into wine. He did not realise where it had come from, though the servants who had drawn the water knew. Then he called the bridegroom aside and said, 'Everyone brings out the choice wine first and then the cheaper wine after the guests have had too much to drink; but you have saved the best till now.'

(John 2:1–10)

For many Christians, marriage and the family lie at the centre of their religious teaching.

In the marriage service of the Church of England, the bride and groom make a number of vows to each other:

I, [the person's name], take you, [the other person's name],
to be my wife [or husband],
to have and to hold
from this day forward;
for better, for worse,
for richer, for poorer,
in sickness and in health,
to love and to cherish,
till death us do part,
according to God's holy law;
and this is my solemn vow.

These vows are the promises which people make to one another about the way in which they will each treat the other person once they are married. Until recently, the bride also promised to obey her husband, but now bride and groom usually make the same set of vows.

The minister who is conducting the service explains why marriage is so important:

- Marriage is a gift from God because he intended men and women to live together
- Men and women should help and support one another and be faithful
- Marriage is for bringing up children

The couple are also warned that they should not enter into marriage 'carelessly, lightly, or selfishly, but reverently, responsibly and after serious thought'.

Marriages, whether they are religious or civil, have to take place in front of witnesses. The witnesses are there to see that the ceremony takes place and that both people are getting married of their own free will. This free will is stressed in the Roman Catholic marriage ceremony where the priest says to the couple to be married:

And so, in the presence of the Church, I ask you to state you intentions:
Are you ready freely and without reservation to give yourselves to each other in marriage?
Are you ready to love and honour each other as man and wife for the rest of your lives?
Are you ready to accept children lovingly from God, and bring them up according to the law of Christ and his Church?

The importance of marriage is stressed by Jesus in the gospels:

A Peasant Wedding, *Brueghel, Pieter the elder (1515–69)*

But from the beginning of creation, God made them male and female. For this reason a man shall leave his father and mother and be joined to his wife, and the two shall become one flesh. So they are no longer two, but one flesh. Therefore what God has joined together, let no one separate.

(Mark 10:6-9)

Jesus taught that divorce is wrong. In the Sermon on the Mount he explained that even the laws about divorce in the Old Testament were not as strict as the ones God wanted:

'It was also said, "Whoever divorces his wife, let him give her a certificate of divorce." But I say to you that anyone who divorces his wife, except on the ground of unchastity, causes her to commit adultery; and whoever marries a divorced woman commits adultery.'

(Matthew 5:31-32)

This text is sometimes used to argue that divorced people should not be allowed to remarry. Divorce is certainly not welcomed in Christianity, but it is permitted in most Churches. In the Roman Catholic Church, however, divorce is not allowed. Sometimes people are given an **annulment** which means that their marriage is considered to never have taken place.

Since 1981 the Church of England has agreed to allow divorced people to remarry. Most Protestant Churches also follow this view, believing that people should not be forced to live alone for the rest of their lives when there may be the opportunity of happiness for them in a new marriage.

Some Christians tolerate the idea of people cohabiting, although they do not generally welcome this. The Roman Catholic Church is completely opposed to cohabitation: the sexual act must take place exclusively within marriage. Sexual intercourse outside marriage always constitutes a grave sin and excludes a person from sacramental communion.

A bride and groom signing the wedding register.

Some couples now claim the right to a trial marriage where there is an intention of getting married later. However, the Catholic Church's view is that such liaisons cannot ensure mutual sincerity and fidelity in a relationship.

A number of the Protestant Churches accept that cohabitation is seen as an option for many people today. Although they may welcome people who live in this sort of relationship into their communities, they still believe that living together outside of marriage is falling short of what God wanted.

All Christian groups stress that whatever the circumstances of a relationship, marriage or divorce, one of the primary concerns of the people involved must be the welfare of their children.

The Muslim marriage ceremony is very simple. There is a declaration to the witnesses of the marriage that the bride and groom are marrying of their own free will. A marriage contract is then signed specifying the **mahr** (dowry) which the groom is giving to the bride. There are prayers and readings and a ceremonial sermon usually led by the imam.

Almighty God created humanity, male and female, each in need of the other, and established the institution of marriage as a means of uniting souls in blessed bond of love, leading to their pleasure and happiness in a way advantageous to mankind. In His Holy Book our Lord says:

'It is He Who has created man from water, and made him kindred of blood and marriage. Your Lord is All Powerful. Brothers and sisters at this precious and auspicious moment, we are uniting in the bond of marriage in obedience to the practice of the beloved Prophet (pbuh) our Brother... and Sister... who have decided to live together as husband and wife, sheltered with the blessing of Almighty Allah and His Divine Benevolence. May Allah fill their life with joy and may He grant them peace, health and prosperity. May they always live together in an atmosphere of peace and tranquillity and never diminishing love and tender regard for each other.'

Some Muslims in the United Kingdom now include specific vows in their marriage ceremony and these include promising that, in accordance with the teaching of the Qur'an, they will work to make the marriage an act of obedience to Allah and a relationship of mercy, love, peace and faithfulness.

Although a Muslim marriage should be supported by Islam and a common belief between the couple, Muslims realise that sometimes marriages breakdown. Marriage is a legal contract between two people and therefore it can be ended. This is done if continuation of the marriage brings misery to the couple, to their children and to close relatives.

In the Hadith it says: 'Among all lawful things, divorce is most hated by Allah'. However the important thing is that divorce is lawful, it is not forbidden by Islam.

The Qur'an says that:

If a wife fears cruelty or desertion on her husband's part, there is no blame on them if they arrange an amicable settlement between themselves; and such settlement is best.

(Surah 4:128)

A man cannot seek a divorce from his wife until it is certain that she is not pregnant as it is possible that he might then change his mind. Once the divorce is announced there is a period of three months called **'iddah**. This is a period in which reconciliation should be attempted. If there is no reconciliation then the divorce takes place. A man and a woman can remarry each other twice, but after a third divorce

The nature of marriage is laid down in the Qur'an:

Among His signs is this, that He created you from dust; and then, – behold, ye are men scattered (far and wide)! He has created for you mates from among yourselves, that ye may dwell in tranquillity with them, and He has put love and mercy between your (hearts): verily in that are Signs for those who reflect.

(Surah 30:20–21)

They are your garments and ye are their garments.

(Surah 2:187)

remarriage to each other cannot take place unless the woman has been married to another man in the meanwhile.

> *So, if a husband divorces his wife (irrevocably), he cannot, after that, re-marry her until after she has married another husband and he has divorced her. In that case there is no blame on either of them if they re-unite, provided they feel that they can keep the limits ordained by God, which he makes plain to those who understand. When ye divorce women, and they fulfil the term of their ('Iddat), either take them back on equitable terms or set them free on equitable terms; but do not take them back to injure them, (or) to take undue advantage; if any one does that, he wrongs his own soul. Do not treat God's signs as a jest, but solemnly rehearse God's favours on you, and the fact that He sent down to you the Book and Wisdom, for your instruction.*

(Surah 2:230–231)

The wife can free herself completely from the marriage by returning her mahr. During the period of 'iddah, she must stay in her husband's house and he must provide everything for her. He is not allowed to evict her. It is hoped that, in this way, there may eventually be a reconciliation.

> *O Prophet! When ye do divorce women, divorce them at their prescribed periods, and count (accurately) their prescribed periods: and fear God your Lord: and turn them not out of their houses, nor shall they (themselves) leave, except in case they are guilty of some open lewdness, those are limits set by God: and any who transgresses the limits of God, does verily wrong his (own) soul: Thou knowest not if perchance God will bring about thereafter some new situation.*

(Surah 65:1)

A woman is able to obtain a divorce, either by an agreement with her husband (khul) or because of his treatment of her. Children are regarded as illegitimate if their parents are not married and according to Shari'ah, the father has no legal responsibility.

As in Judaism, Muslims have rules about 'marrying out' of the religion. A Muslim man may marry a Jewish or Christian woman but a Muslim woman is forbidden to marry anyone except a Muslim.

Divorce document

Marriage certificate

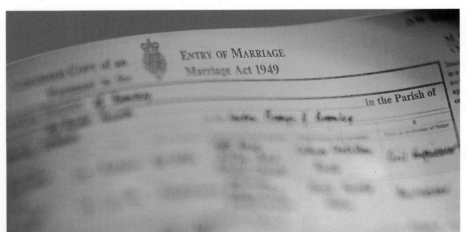

Summary

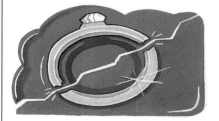

It might seem that each of these three religions have strict rules about marriage and divorce. Perhaps this shows just how important marriage and the family are for believers of these faiths.

Jews, Christians and Muslims all believe that the family is central to their religion and to the way in which God means them to live. Because of this, they all have ceremonies to bless a marriage and they all have rules about divorce which make it difficult for people to separate and remain within the religion. These rules are intended to make people think very carefully before they are married and also to try very hard to make marriage work.

It is also clear that all three religions believe that people who wish to live together in a sexual relationship should be married and should not simply cohabit.

1 What do you understand by:

marriage and divorce

civil marriage

cohabitation

illegitimate

dowry?

2 Why do you think the number of people getting divorced is rising so quickly?

3 Consider whether people have really changed their attitude towards marriage and cohabitation.

4 Explain why religious people may not want their son or daughter to marry someone who belongs to a different religion.

5 Explain how these religions treat men and women over the question of divorce.

6 Do you think that religions and society treat illegitimate children differently? Explain your opinion about this.

7 Consider the statement that 'marriage is simply out of date now, people should just live together'.

The followers of Judaism, Christianity and Islam say that they believe in one God and that this is a good God who would want everyone to be happy, safe and contented in their earthly life. As God wants a good life for everyone, each religion teaches that its followers should work to make the world a better place.

It is difficult then, for religious people to accept a world where many people are poor and suffering. People in developing countries are often deprived, not only of a high standard of living, but also of modern medical care and attention. Each religion teaches that this is wrong and that everyone should benefit from what is often called 'God's bounty'.

In the past, some religions have invested money in countries and industries which exploit people and treat them in a way which is completely against the teachings of the religion.

Today most people think that this was wrong and that religions should work towards ending poverty and helping people to improve their living standards. They would also argue that everyone should be treated equally.

Central to this discussion is the Universal Declaration of Human Rights which was signed by the General Assembly of the United Nations on 10 December 1948. This laid out the basic rights to which the people of the world should be entitled. Most important for us, perhaps, is the First Article of the Declaration which says:

All human beings are born free and equal in dignity and rights. They are endowed with reason and conscience and should act towards one another in a spirit of brotherhood.

Sometimes people may find that the wish or desire to have something may put them into conflict with what their religion teaches. The Tenth Commandment is central to this way of thinking:

You shall not covet your neighbour's house. You shall not covet your neighbour's wife, or his manservant or maidservant, his ox or donkey, or anything that belongs to your neighbour.

(Exodus 20:17)

Religious people must also think about the way in which they lead their lives at work and ask themselves whether they are behaving honestly and properly towards others, as their religion teaches.

People living on a rubbish dump in the Philippines.

Preamble to the Universal Declaration of Human Rights

Whereas recognition of the inherent dignity and of the equal and inalienable rights of all members of the human family is the foundation of freedom, justice and peace in the world,
Whereas disregard and contempt for human rights have resulted in barbarous acts which have outraged the conscience of mankind, and the advent of a world in which human beings shall enjoy freedom of speech and belief and freedom from fear and want has been proclaimed as the highest aspiration of the common people,
…
Whereas the peoples of the United Nations have in the Charter reaffirmed their faith in fundamental human rights, in the dignity and worth of the human person and in the equal rights of men and women and have determined to promote social progress and better standards of life in larger freedom.

Jewish teaching on poverty and wealth can be found in the Tenakh.

Jews are expected to give a tenth of their wealth as **tzedaka** (righteousness). This money is owing to the poor, and not to give it is to rob them. Even the very poorest people should try to give something as tzedaka.

According to Judaism, the worst way to give tzedaka is to hand someone the money; the best way is to lend it to them indefinitely and without interest. It teaches that by doing so, you are saving people the embarrassment of taking a gift. The hope is that the money will help a poor person to become self-supporting.

> *The best way of giving is to help a person help themselves so that they may become self-supporting*
>
> (Maimonides)

> *If there is a poor man among your brothers in any of the towns of the land that the Lord your God is giving you, do not be hard-hearted or tight-fisted towards your poor brother. Rather be open-handed and freely lend him whatever he needs.*
>
> (Deuteronomy 19:9–10)

At home, many Jews have collection boxes called **pushkes** and children are encouraged to use these so that they can give part of their pocket money to charity.

As well as tzedaka, Jews should try to ensure that any excess wealth is also used for the poor:

> *When you reap the harvest of your land, do not reap to the very edges of your field or gather the gleanings of your harvest. Do not go over your vineyard a second time or pick up the grapes that have fallen. Leave them for the poor and the alien.*
>
> (Leviticus 19:9–10)

The Talmud teaches that people must never seek to make themselves poor. This is wrong because it makes other people then become responsible for you.

> *It is better to make your Sabbath like a weekday than to need other people's support.*

Although Judaism believes that it is wrong to make yourself poor it is totally opposed to materialism.

> *Do not wear yourself out to get rich; have the wisdom to show restraint.*
>
> (Proverbs 23:4)

> *Whoever loves money never has money enough; whoever loves wealth is never satisfied with his income.*
>
> (Ecclesiastes 5:10)

Love of money can eventually lead people away from God:

> *Be careful that you do not forget the Lord your God, failing to observe his commands, his laws and his decrees that I am giving you this day. Otherwise, when you eat and are satisfied, when you build fine houses and settle down, and when your herds and flocks grow large and your silver and gold increase and all you have is multiplied, then your heart will become proud and you will forget the Lord your God, who brought you out of Egypt, out of the land of slavery.*
>
> (Deuteronomy 8:11-14)

Gemilut Hasadim is another form of Jewish charity. Literally it means 'kind actions' and covers all sorts of charitable work. It might be organisations for Jews such as Jewish Care or the Norwood Orphanages, soup kitchens to feed the hungry and homeless, or more global organisations such as Tzedek which works to improve conditions for all people around the world.

One of the most important aspects of Jewish working life is Shabbat, the Sabbath, on which no work is done.

> *'Remember the Sabbath day by keeping it holy. Six days you shall labour and do all your work, but the seventh day is a Sabbath to the Lord your God. On it you shall not do any work, neither you, nor your son or daughter, nor your manservant or maidservant, nor your animals, nor the alien within your gates. For in six days the Lord made the heavens and the earth, the sea, and all that is in them, but he rested on the seventh day. Therefore the Lord blessed the Sabbath day and made it holy.'*
>
> (Exodus 20:8-10)

The Rabbis laid down 39 different types of forbidden activities for the Sabbath. These include all work, writing, cooking and travel, except on foot. The only time on which these laws can be broken is in the case of **pikuakh nefesh**. This mitzvah means that almost any law can be broken in order to save life:

> *Whoever destroys a single life is considered as if he had destroyed the whole world, and whoever saves a single life as if he had saved the whole world.*
>
> (Mishnah)

Jews are not breaking the sanctity of the Sabbath if they ask someone to do a task for them on that day. Non-Jews, who are not bound by the Sabbath rules, can work for Jews on the Sabbath if the arrangement is made beforehand.

Everyone is expected to work as it is an essential part of Jewish life:

> By the sweat of your brow you will eat your food until you return to the ground, since from it you were taken; for dust you are and to dust you will return.
>
> (Genesis 3:19)

> Great is work. God's presence only rested upon the Jewish people when they began occupying themselves with useful work.
>
> (Maimonides).

Jewish teaching, however, stresses that work should also allow time for Torah study. Jewish law requires that all business transactions are honest:

> Do not use dishonest standards when measuring length, weight or quantity. Use honest scales and honest weights, an honest ephah [19.7 litres] and an honest hin [3.7 litres].
>
> (Leviticus 19:35)

A family gathered for Shabbat.

'No one can serve two masters. Either he will hate the one and love the other, or he will be devoted to the one and despise the other. You cannot serve both God and Money.

'Therefore I tell you, do not worry about your life, what you will eat or drink; or about your body, what you will wear. Is not life more important than food, and the body more important than clothes? Look at the birds of the air; they do not sow or reap or store away in barns, and yet your heavenly Father feeds them. Are you not much more valuable than they? Who of you by worrying can add a single hour to his life?

'And why do you worry about clothes? See how the lilies of the field grow. They do not labour or spin. Yet I tell you that not even Solomon in all his splendour was dressed like one of these. If that is how God clothes the grass of the field, which is here today and tomorrow is thrown into the fire, will he not much more clothe you, O you of little faith? So do not worry, saying, "What shall we eat?" or "What shall we drink?" or "What shall we wear?"'

(Matthew 6:24–31)

Christianity has many teachings which are to do with the treatment of other people. It could be said that the Second Commandment which Jesus gave to his disciples lies at the centre of all Christian teaching:

'Love the Lord your God with all your heart and with all your soul and with all your mind and with all your strength.' The second is this: 'Love your neighbour as yourself.' There is no commandment greater than these.

(Mark 12:30–31)

Jesus explained to his followers that they should give away their riches in order to follow God. He said that:

'it is easier for a camel to go through the eye of a needle than for a rich man to enter the kingdom of God.'

(Luke 18:25)

He also taught that people should look after one another:

'For I was hungry and you gave me something to eat, I was thirsty and you gave me something to drink, I was a stranger and you invited me in, I needed clothes and you clothed me, I was sick and you looked after me, I was in prison and you came to visit me.'

(Matthew 25:35–36)

The first Christians followed his teachings according to the Acts of the Apostles:

All the believers were together and had everything in common. Selling their possessions and goods, they gave to anyone as he had need.

(Acts 2:44–45)

Today, as the world seems to become more and more secular, many people feel that making money is the main purpose of their lives. The enormous success of the National Lottery and of 'scratch cards' in the United Kingdom shows how much people want money, but this goes against Christian teaching:

People who want to get rich fall into temptation and a trap and into many foolish and harmful desires that plunge men into ruin and destruction. For the love of money is a root of all kinds of evil. Some people, eager for money, have wandered from the faith and pierced themselves with many griefs.

(I Timothy 6:9–10)

The Second Vatican Council of the Roman Catholic Church said that there was no separation between the religious and the secular world; it is all God's. Therefore faith and justice are linked together. The Catechism of the Catholic Church says

True happiness is not found in riches or well-being, in human fame or power, or in any human achievement… God blesses those who come to the aid of the poor and rebukes those who turn away from them.

It continues by stressing that:

> *Rich nations have a grave moral responsibility towards those which are unable to ensure the means of their development by themselves.*

In recent years the Christian Churches have concerned themselves more with issues such as poverty and the fairer distribution of wealth in the world. It is not correct to say simply that some countries are overpopulated, the truth is that a few very rich nations hold most of the world's wealth and that resources of both money and food are not distributed equally.

Charities such as Christian Aid, CAFOD and the TEAR Fund have been set up to co-ordinate the work of the Churches and to try to ensure that millions of people are not left starving.

In 1981 the General Synod of the Church of England said:

> the Synod [believes] that, as a matter of common humanity and of our mutual interest in survival, the world requires a new and more equitable system of economic relationships between nations.

Christians have a duty to ensure that the way in which they earn their living does not have a bad affect on other people. You could argue, therefore, that Christians should not be involved in the arms trade, in prostitution or pornography.

In recent years the law in the United Kingdom has been changed so that all shops can open on a Sunday. Some Christians have said that this breaks the Fourth Commandment:

> *Remember the Sabbath day by keeping it holy. Six days you shall labour and do all your work, but the seventh day is a Sabbath to the Lord your God. On it you shall not do any work, neither you, nor your son or daughter, nor your manservant or maidservant, nor your animals, nor the alien within your gates. For in six days the Lord made the heavens and the earth, the sea, and all that is in them, but he rested on the seventh day. Therefore the Lord blessed the Sabbath day and made it holy.*
>
> (Exodus 20:8)

Statue of Christ the Redeemer, Rio de Janeiro

One modern development which is particularly concerned with the issues of equality for all people is Liberation Theology. This idea has followers from both the Protestant and Roman Catholic Churches. It is a belief that people who follow Jesus' teachings must take positive action to fight against social injustice and the misuse of power by governments. Liberation Theology is particularly strong amongst the priests in Latin America and parts of Asia and Africa. If the law acts against ordinary people in a way which is un-Christian, these people believe that they have a duty to oppose and, if necessary, break the law.

> *'The Spirit of the Lord is on me, because he has anointed me to preach good news to the poor. He has sent me to proclaim freedom for the prisoners and recovery of sight for the blind, to release the oppressed'*
>
> (Luke 4:18)

To Muslims, all wealth and riches come from Allah and are for the benefit of all humanity. Central to Islamic belief in this matter is **zakah** (purification of wealth by payment of welfare due) which is one of the Five Pillars:

And be steadfast in prayer and regular in charity: and whatever good ye send forth for your souls before you, ye shall find it with God: for God sees well all that ye do.

(Surah 2:111)

Zakah 'purifies' the wealth that Muslims have so that no harm can come to them from it. Zakah itself is 2.5 per cent of the income and savings of all Muslims after they have taken care of their families. It is not a charitable donation which people can choose to make, but an obligation on all Muslims, however rich or poor they are. In an Islamic state, zakah is a form of social security; it ensures that food, clothing, housing, medicine and education can be provided for every person.

Alms are for the poor and the needy, and those employed to administer the (funds); for those whose hearts have been (recently) reconciled (to Truth); for those in bondage and in debt; in the cause of God; and for the wayfarer.

(Surah 9:60)

Extra zakah is given at the festivals of Id-ul-Fitr and Id-ul-Adha. Additional voluntary charity, called **sadaqah**, can also be given when someone is in need.

It is not righteousness that ye turn your faces towards East or West; but it is righteousness – to believe in God and the Last Day, and the Angels, and the Book, and the Messengers; to spend of your substance, out of love for Him, for your kin, for orphans, for the needy, for the wayfarer, for those who ask, and for the ransom of slaves; to be steadfast in prayer, and practice regular charity; to fulfil the contracts which ye have made; and to be firm and patient, in pain (or suffering) and adversity and throughout all periods of panic. Such are the people of truth, the God-fearing.

(Surah 2:177)

Because of their beliefs, Muslims in the United Kingdom take an active part in raising money for their mosque. The money is then distributed to the poor and many will send money to Muslim communities abroad. Muslim charities such as Muslim Aid and Islamic Relief work to help people in developing countries.

The generous man is near God, near Paradise, near men and far from Hell, and the ignorant man who is generous is dearer to God than a worshipper who is miserly.

(Hadith)

According to Islam, charity should be done privately:

There is a man who gives charity and he conceals it so much that his left hand does not know what his right hand spends.

(Hadith)

Benefiting from **Riba** (interest) is forbidden:

That which ye lay out for increase through the property of (other) people, will have no increase with God.

(Surah 30:39)

Muslims are encouraged to be sympathetic to a debtor:

If the debtor is in a difficulty, grant him time till it is easy for him to repay. But if ye remit it by way of charity, that is best for you if ye only knew.

(Surah 2:280)

As well as interest, all forms of gambling and lotteries are forbidden in Islam:

O ye who believe! Intoxicants and gambling, (dedication of) stones, and (divination by) arrows, are an abomination, – of Satan's handiwork.

(Surah 5:93)

Work is an essential part of Islamic life. This is stressed in the Qur'an, as are those ways in which Muslims should not earn their living:

But God has created you and your handiwork!

(Surah 37:96)

Muslims cannot earn their living from alcohol or gambling, from brothels or prostitution:

Women impure and for men impure, and men impure for women impure and women of purity are for men of purity, and men of purity are for women of purity.

(Surah 24:26)

Nor from lying, fraud or burglary:

And do not eat up your property among yourselves for vanities, nor use it as bait for the judges, with intent that ye may eat up wrongfully and knowingly a little of (other) people's property.

(Surah 2:188)

The two Pillars of Salah (prayer) and Sawm (fasting from sunrise to sunset through the month of Ramadan) are also important elements in Muslim teaching about work.

Praying five times a day at fixed times means that work is put into perspective when Muslims stop their normal activities to think about Allah. This is particularly true of Salat-ul-Jumu'ah, the weekly prayers at noon on Fridays.

Islam does not have a day of rest, but all Muslims try to attend these prayers each Friday and hear the **Khutbah** (talk) given by the imam. In a similar way, the fast of Ramadan brings people closer together in **Ummah** (the world Islamic community) and helps them to focus on God when they are also controlling their bodies.

Muslim and Christian aid agencies in Seville.

Summary

Although their practices may be different, each of these three religions stress the importance of equality and they could all be said to be working towards the First Article of the Declaration of Human Rights:

All human beings are born free and equal in dignity and rights. They are endowed with reason and conscience and should act towards one another in a spirit of brotherhood.

They all believe that wealth should be fairly distributed and that they should work, not only to support their families, but also to help those who are less fortunate. It is by doing this that they reflect God's love for them and for all humanity.

1 What do you understand by:

Human Rights

charity

materialism

interest

the Developing World

Liberation Theology?

2 The Declaration of Human Rights was written in 1948. Do you think there are still things that religious believers can do to make it work?

3 How far do you think religion should 'interfere' in the way in which business is done?

4 Explain how people might decide how much of their money they should keep and how much they should give to charity.

5 Explain why some people might say that it is wrong to take part in a public lottery.

6 Consider whether people should take a more active part in helping others as Liberation Theology proposes.

7 Some people say that being poor is a person's own fault and that they should solve their own problems. Explain how you would react to this idea.

In this chapter we will be looking at the way in which religions and religious issues are presented in the media.

In the past, people learned about their religion from their families, by reading or listening to their sacred texts and by going to a place of worship. Today many people find out more about religion from the media than from anywhere else.

Fewer people attend places of worship regularly than they did in the past. This does not necessarily mean that less people believe in religion, but it does imply that many people no longer feel that it is important to attend religious services.

Between 1975 and 1990 the membership of Christian churches in the United Kingdom fell by one-sixth (over one million), although membership of Muslim and Sikh places of worship increased by 764,000 and of Mormons and Jehovah's Witnesses by 85,000. These numbers are continuing to move in the same directions.

The media

The Oxford English Dictionary says that the media is: *Newspapers, radio, television, etc., collectively, as vehicles of mass communication.*

Media can be television, video, radio, newspapers, magazines, books, advertisements, computers and the Internet and some types of music.

People have said that the media is a bad influence on life today and that young people especially are misled by television and other forms of

entertainment. At some time or another the media has been blamed for almost every social ill. The bulk of television output is secular (i.e. not religious) and we have all seen and heard people complaining that there is too much pornography and too much violence on television, even before the so-called 9pm 'watershed' when it is assumed that young children will have gone to bed.

Jews and Christians are supposed to give a tenth of their income to their religion:

A tithe of everything from the land, whether grain from the soil or fruit from the trees, belongs to the Lord; it is holy to the Lord. If a man redeems any of his tithe, he must add a fifth of the value to it. The entire tithe of the herd and flock – every tenth animal that passes under the shepherd's rod – will be holy to the Lord. He must not pick out the good from the bad or make any substitution. If he does make a substitution, both the animal and its substitute become holy and cannot be redeemed.
(Leviticus 27:30-33)

...you give God a tenth of your mint, rue and all other kinds of garden herbs, but you neglect justice and the love of God. You should have practised the latter without leaving the former undone.
(Luke 11:42)

Therefore, in 1993, an 'average' Christian or Jewish family with two children should have been giving between £17.50 and £43.50 towards their religion every week.

Muslims are required to give **zakah** (purification of wealth by the payment of an annual welfare due).

And be steadfast in prayer and regular in charity: and whatever good ye send forth for your souls before you, ye shall find it with God.
(Surah 2:110)

Today, most people spend a great deal of money on the media in the United Kingdom:

1960	10½ million television licences were issued
1977	18 million television licences were issued
1993	people watched an average of 25¾ hours of television every week, equivalent to over 3½ hours a day
1993	27½ million people read at least one daily newspaper every day
1993	30 million read a Sunday paper
1995	95 million CDs were sold
1995	58 million cassette tapes were sold
1995	58 million singles were sold

This means that in 1995, each household in the country spent an average of £10.53 a week on these various types of media. These activities are of increasing importance in our lives while, for many people, going to a place of worship becomes less and less important or at least, less frequent.

The TV listings on the right shows a typical Sunday's broadcasting on radio and television (both BBC and ITV) in the London area during 1996. This is a total of ten hours and fifty minutes of which one hour was devoted to Judaism and no time to any other non-Christian religion. The satellite channels did not broadcast any programmes with a religious content. The total broadcasting time on that day was 188 hours and 40 minutes. So, on this particular Sunday, 5.7 per cent of broadcasting was related to religious issues.

Television and radio have always had an important role in bringing religious programmes and issues to the public. When the BBC started regular television broadcasting in 1946 it concentrated on religious programmes on Sundays between 10:30am and 12 noon and from 6.00pm until 7.00pm (2½ hours). These times became known as the 'God–Slot' and were almost always of entirely Christian content. This has changed in recent years, but although there is now far less specifically religious broadcasting, there are many programmes which have a clear religious content.

Presenters of BBC TV's Songs of Praise *on its 35th anniversary in 1996.*

Time	Channel	Programme
05:50-06:00	R4	**Bells on Sunday**
06:30-06:40	ITV	**Matter of Faith**
06:30-08:00	GLR	**Gospel Show**
07:40-08:50	R4	**Sunday** religious news
09:30-09.45	BBC1	**Heart to Heart** people who claim to have 'heart to hearts' with God.
09:30-10:15	R4	**Morning Service** from Paisley
09:45-10:15	BBC1	**First Light** a series looking at people's ideas of heaven
10:30-11:30	ITV	**Morning Worship** from Aberdeen
11:30-11:50	ITV	**Heavenly Voices** an exploration of the history of church music
11:50-12:30	ITV	**Many Questions** ethical and moral dilemmas
16:35-17:35	C4	**Why East Grinstead?** A look at the religious life of the town
17:00-18:00	R2	**Roger Royle**
18:05-18:40	BBC1	**Songs of Praise** from Newquay
20:30-21:00	R2	**Sunday Half Hour**
21:00-22:00	GLR	**Jewish London**
23:45-12:00	R4	**Seeds of Faith**

Whether you think that there is too little or too much religious broadcasting will probably depend on your personal beliefs. We have been looking at the time given to religious broadcasting, but perhaps more important are the other types of broadcasting which take place. Much of the religious content on television comes within documentary and drama programmes rather than in those which are designed specifically as some form of worship.

One of the standard film encyclopaedias lists only 77 mainstream films as religious. The television companies do sometimes show films such as *The Ten Commandments* and *Jesus of Nazareth* but usually only on Christian religious holidays. *The Message*, a film about the life of the Prophet Muhammad, has never been shown on British television.

Educational television has always had specifically religious programmes such as *Believe it or Not* and programmes which deal with ethical issues like *Scene*.

The major television channels and some radio programmes broadcast documentaries about religions and religious issues. In recent years these have included programmes on Amish, Buddhism, Christianity, Gnosticism, Hinduism, Hutterites, Islam, Jainism, Judaism, Moonies, Paganism, Rastafarianism, Scientology, Sikhism and Zoroastrianism.

Additionally, there are a number of regular documentary programmes which deal with religious issues. These include *Everyman* and *Heart of the Matter* from the BBC and *Witness* on C4. They have covered issues such as women priests, homosexuality, euthanasia, abortion and adoption as well as more specialised matters such as the Shroud of Turin, the role of missionaries, biblical archaeology, Liberation theology, the life of monks and nuns, and the pyramids of Egypt. One of the most successful religious programmes of recent years has been the *Moral Maze*. This began on BBC Radio and then transferred to television. It is concerned with giving the opportunity for religious discussion about some of the moral dilemmas facing people today.

Secular programmes

Two of the most popular forms of entertainment on the television are science fiction and soap operas.

Science fiction has become increasingly popular over recent years and many programmes have achieved cult status. In particular, the *X Files* which has dealt with many fringe 'religious' issues such as aliens and the paranormal, and *Star Trek*.

Star Trek began as an American television series in the 1960s and its success has been world-wide. It has developed into an enormous industry, producing other series, movies, books, computer games and merchandise but also giving rise to a lot of serious discussion about the ideas explored in the series. It may seem that science fiction is all about special effects and fighting off aliens, but many of the issues raised deal

Joan Bakewell presenter of BBC TV's Heart of the Matter

Brookside, *Channel 4*

with the same fundamental questions of life as this Religious Education course. These include ideas such as:

Is there a God?
Why are we here?
How did we get here?
What happens to us when we die?
What do we mean by life and how should we treat other human and non-human forms of life?
Do we have the right to interfere in other people's lives?

Star Trek has also dealt with issues of prejudice; not assuming that people who look different from us are inferior to us; and whether or not things or people actually 'belong' to other people. Although an answer may not be produced to a particular question, viewers are nevertheless left considering at least a humanitarian response to the issue.

In the same week in which we looked at religious broadcasting on a Sunday, the four main television channels broadcast 16 hours of soap operas: these included *Brookside, Coronation Street, EastEnders, Emmerdale Farm, Home and Away* and *Neighbours*. In addition, BBC Radio had four hours and twenty minutes of the *Archers* which is broadcast six days a week and has been running since 1951.

People might say that these programmes are just rather silly escapism: 'trash TV'. However, because the characters' lives are squashed into a few hours each week and because people like to be able to identify with them, these programmes deal with many questions which concern all of us at some time.

The soaps have all covered general issues such as birth, marriage, illness and death as well as ideas such as jealousy, envy, greed, human weaknesses, sexism and racism. They have also dealt with many other current topics: Down's Syndrome, women priests, homosexuality, lesbianism, drugs, illegitimate children, adultery and incest. These programmes do not teach us how we should deal with these matters but they do give us the opportunity, in a safe environment, to see some of the ways in which people behave and how they address these issues. They can also be responsible for helping people to look again at some issues: the way in which the characters in *EastEnders* have dealt with Mark Fowler being HIV Positive; the Jordache family in *Brookside* who had to cope with wife-battering, murder, lesbianism and imprisonment; *Neighbours* has raised questions about relationships both married and unmarried, sudden deaths, and Mark Gottlieb believing he had a vocation to the priesthood and changing his mind again; finally, *Home and Away* has covered leukaemia, abortion, unemployment and many issues about honesty and relationships.

Eastenders, *BBC*

The written word

Books have always been important for religion. These not only include sacred texts such as the Bible or the Qur'an, but also novels such as *The Pilgrim's Progress* by John Bunyan or, more generally, *Aesop's Fables*.

Almost half the population of the United Kingdom read at least one daily newspaper. Religion does get some coverage in newspapers, but usually only when something 'sensational' happens such as a clergyman being accused of adultery. It is unlikely that people will acquire very informed religious or ethical opinions from the 'Shock Horror', 'Outrage', 'This must be stopped' kind of headlines which tend to appear in the most popular daily papers.

Sometimes one form of media or another will print or broadcast something which religious people find very offensive. Offensive or abusive remarks about God are called **blasphemy**.

In the 1970s the newspaper *Gay News* published a poem by the American writer James Kirkup which suggested that Jesus might have been homosexual. The Courts said that it was blasphemous to publish such a poem and the editor of the newspaper was prosecuted. However, when in the 1980s the writer Salman Rushdie wrote *The Satanic Verses* which caused offence to many Muslims the Courts decided that, in England, blasphemy only offered protection to Christianity and possibly only to the Church of England.

An illustration from The Pilgrim's Progress, *John Bunyan.*

A Muslim protest against the publication of The Satanic Verses.

There are references to blasphemy in the Jewish scriptures with very specific punishments:

> Then the Lord said to Moses: 'Take the blasphemer outside the camp. All those who heard him are to lay their hands on his head, and the entire assembly is to stone him. Say to the Israelites: "If anyone curses his God, he will be held responsible; anyone who blasphemes the name of the Lord must be put to death."'
>
> (Leviticus 24:13–16)

Jesus of Nazareth was accused of blasphemy at his trial because he was said to have claimed to be the Messiah:

> Again the high priest asked him, 'Are you the Christ, the Son of the Blessed One?' 'I am,' said Jesus. 'And you will see the Son of Man sitting at the right hand of the Mighty One and coming on the clouds of heaven.' The high priest tore his clothes. 'Why do we need any more witnesses?' he asked. 'You have heard the blasphemy. What do you think?' They all condemned him as worthy of death.
>
> (Mark 14:61–64)

Blasphemy is also against the teachings of Islam which requires its followers to always tell the truth about God:

> And shun the word that is false, being true in faith to God, and never assigning partners to Him: if anyone assigns partners to God, he is as if he had fallen from heaven and been snatched up by birds, or the wind had swooped (like a bird on its prey) and thrown him into a far-distant place.
>
> (Surah 22:30-31)

If you love your children, butter them up.

It takes the cream from 18 pints of milk to make one pound of butter. The best taste in the world for just a few pennies more than margarine.

We're all a lot better for butter.

Music

Music is another form of media which occupies a great deal of people's time.

The music which we normally associate with the media is probably pop music and this is unlikely to have much religious content. Almost all pop songs are about love and love affairs, about happiness and unhappiness. While these ideas are very important to many people, they tend to be handled in a way which makes love and, particularly, sex seem the most important aspects of life and things which we must all try to achieve whatever the cost.

The three religions which we are considering have all, at one time or another, disapproved of the sentiments of some pop music. Christianity has a long tradition of religious music which is used as part of many services, but has gone some way to using the forms and sound of pop music in worship in order to try to make it more relevant to young people.

Music is also an important aspect of Jewish worship. Because of the restrictions about work on the Sabbath, no musical instruments can be used in these services and the singing is therefore unaccompanied.

Many Muslims are opposed to any kind of music because the Prophet Muhammad said:

> *There will be at some future time people from my nation who will seek to make lawful, adultery, the wearing of silk by men, wine-drinking and the use of musical instruments.*

> (Hadith)

Other Muslims have no objection to the use of music provided that it does not encourage unsuitable thoughts or actions.

Advertising

Advertising is one aspect of the media which we encounter every day. Most adverts are designed to make us want things and so to buy them. We are all told that we will be happier, more successful, sexier or healthier if we buy a particular product and this might be anything from yoghurt to alcohol, cigarettes or a new car. Advertising is not generally trying to inform us about things, instead it tries to make us want them and in doing so it encourages us all to break the Tenth Commandment of Judaism and Christianity:

> *You shall not covet your neighbour's house. You shall not covet your neighbour's wife, or his manservant or maidservant, his ox or donkey, or anything that belongs to your neighbour.*

> (Exodus 20:17)

The things which we decide we want may not belong to our 'neighbour' but also they do not belong to us, and the advertising has created a 'need'. There has also been argument between religious groups and advertisers over some of the images which are used in advertisements. In particular this applies to the selling of goods such as alcohol and cigarettes and the use of sex and sexual images to advertise products.

Information Technology

The newest form of media is the computer and, in particular, the Internet. Most schools have a number of computers for students to use and an increasing number of these have access to the Internet, the world-wide communications method which enables people to obtain information from other computers all over the world.

Many religious people see the use of computers as a means of education and of helping people to work more efficiently and more pleasantly. However, one religious group has spoken out against computers. The Exclusive Brethren (part of the Plymouth Brethren, a Christian group who expect the end of the world to come very soon), have said that computers are the work of the devil and have forbidden their use.

The Internet has caused concern amongst people, including religious leaders. The content of it cannot be controlled easily and almost anyone who has the right equipment can put material on to the Internet which can then be accessed by anyone who has a suitable computer system. Most of the publicity in the papers and on the television has been about fears of young children looking at pornography on the Internet, but it is also worrying that there materials which can be found there which encourage racist and sexist attitudes.

A page on Judaism from the Internet.

Andrew Tannenbaum's Judaism and Jewish Resources   http://shamash.nysernet.org/trb/judaism.html

Judaism and Jewish Resources

The Internet is rich with Jewish resources. This page shows you the gates to these resources, so that you may go in and explore.

The latest version of this page may be found at: http://shamash.org/trb/judaism.html

What's new?
About this page.
J&JR Scavenger Hunt.
Jump past table of contents.

Table of Contents

Webs and Gophers	FTP archives
Mailing lists	The State of Israel
News and Media	Usenet
SCJ FAQ & Reading Lists	Lubavitch
Jewish Learning	Products and Services
Jewish Communities	Yiddish
Hebrew	Sephardi
Arts	Museums and Exhibitions
Jewish Organizations	Archeology
Internet Relay Chat	Libraries
Books	Jewish Studies
Calendar	Travels
Kashrut	Holocaust
Singles	Other Index Links
Other Pages	Bottom

Web and Gopher Central Services

Israel is very well connected to the Internet, there are many companies and organizations on the Web, in the public and private sector. This page points to Israeli indexes to keep track of most Israeli sites, rather than trying to duplicate their efforts. The **Israel Sensitive Map** is a graphic interface with pointers to Web and Gopher servers in Israel, at Machba (the Israeli Interuniversity Computer Center - www.il). A text-based list is also available there.

Summary

The media, in its many forms, is part of all our lives whether we like what it presents to us or not. As well as sometimes being a bad influence on people, however, all forms of media can encourage and help people to look at and consider moral, ethical and religious issues.

1 What do you understand by:

the media

religious broadcasting

advertising

the 'God-Slot'

mass communication

tithing?

2 Look at the specifically religious broadcasting on one of the main television channels for a week. Decide what the purpose of the programmes are and who they are aimed at. Do you think that they are appropriate for a country which has the particular religious and cultural mix of the United Kingdom?

3 Check the documentary broadcasting over a month on all the main channels. Make a list of those documentaries which have a religious or ethical subject and ask the same questions again.

4 Watch your favourite soap opera for a week. Write down any ethical or religious ideas which are dealt with. Say how well you think these were handled and how 'correct' the characters' behaviour and decisions were.

5 Explain which part of the media, in your opinion, has most to contribute towards religious and moral issues and which has least. You should produce evidence to support your opinions.

6 If you were given ten hours of television and radio time to fill on a Sunday with 'religious' programmes, what would you include?

7 It appears that, in England, the law only protects Christians and that all other religions are excluded. (a) Do you think that this should be changed, and why?
(b) Explain whether you think that all religions should be protected against blasphemy or whether this might interfere with free speech.

13 A four-legged friend

In the 1940s an American actor called Roy Rogers sang about his horse:

A four-legged friend, a four-legged friend,
He'll never let you down
He's honest and faithful right up to the end
That wonderful, one, two, three, four-legged friend.

It has often been said that it is easier to collect money for an animal charity than for one which is concerned with starving or badly treated children. People talk about 'sweet fluffy animals' as though they are toys or babies and 'poor dumb animals' as though they are completely incapable of living on their own. Quite often, it seems that people have a very unrealistic and unnatural attitude towards animals.

Almost everyone would agree that we should not treat animals cruelly. People are shocked when they see pictures released by the RSPCA which show animals covered in sores, and starving to death.

Most people believe that animals should not be harmed unnecessarily, but many also believe that animals should be used in experiments which are considered too dangerous to carry out on human beings. Animals have been used very successfully in many types of medical research. Also, in recent years, there has been widespread protest over the wearing of fur. We must remember, however, that in some countries, such as those in the polar regions, animals are being shot for food and people wear fur coats because it is the only sensible way for them to keep warm.

Throughout the world, animals are bred as a source of food. The majority of the world's people are omnivores, they eat meat, fish, dairy products, and fruit and vegetables. Today, however, more and more people are choosing not to eat meat and to become vegetarians. Some are choosing to become vegans, that is, they will not eat meat or dairy products. There are others who will eat fish, but not other animals. People choose to not eat certain kinds of food for different reasons. From what they choose to give up, it is clear that some people think that certain types of animals should be treated differently.

What is true is that we need some sort of food to live. Some animals eat plants to survive, some eat each other. We have the choice of what we eat.

All of the world's religions have given guidance to their followers about what they should and should not eat.

We are known as a nation of animal lovers and there are many organisations concerned with the care of animals in Britain today. These include:

RSPB   (Royal Society for the Protection of Birds)
RSPCA (Royal Society for the Prevention of Cruelty to Animals)
Greenpeace
World Wildlife Fund

No survey has been carried out on the domestic animal population of the United Kingdom for more than twenty years. The last figures, produced in 1975, showed that nearly a quarter of all homes had at least one pet.

An RSPCA brochure.

RSPCA Campaigns
Veal crates
why they must go.....
RSPCA

The Jewish food rules can be found in the book of Leviticus:

> You may eat any animal that has a split hoof completely divided and that chews the cud.
>
> Of all the creatures living in the water of the seas and the streams, you may eat any that have fins and scales.
>
> These are the birds you are to detest and not eat because they are detestable: the eagle, the vulture, the black vulture, the red kite, any kind of black kite, any kind of raven, the horned owl, the screech owl, the gull, any kind of hawk, the little owl, the cormorant, the great owl, the white owl, the desert owl, the osprey, the stork, any kind of heron, the hoopoe and the bat.
>
> All flying insects that walk on all fours are to be detestable to you. There are, however, some winged creatures that walk on all fours that you may eat: those that have jointed legs for hopping on the ground.
> Every creature that moves about on the ground is detestable; it is not to be eaten. You are not to eat any creature that moves about on the ground, whether it moves on its belly or walks on all fours or on many feet; it is detestable.
>
> (Leviticus 11:3, 9, 13–23, 41–42)

Judaism is the oldest of the three religions which we are considering in this book and its food laws have influenced both Christianity and Islam.

After the creation of the world, God said:

> *'Let us make man in our image, in our likeness, and let them rule over the fish of the sea and the birds of the air, over the livestock, over all the earth, and over all the creatures that move along the ground.'*
>
> (Genesis 1:26)

> *Then God said, 'I give you every seed-bearing plant on the face of the whole earth and every tree that has fruit with seed in it. They will be yours for food.'*
>
> (Genesis 1:29)

At this point, it seems that people were not meant to eat animals. After the flood, however, God told Noah:

> *'Everything that lives and moves will be food for you. Just as I gave you the green plants, I now give you everything. But you must not eat meat that has its lifeblood still in it'.*
>
> (Genesis 9:3–4)

It seems that from this time, God intended people to eat all kinds of meat provided that it did not contain blood.

Later, when the Israelites were in the desert after they had escaped from Egypt, they were given much stricter rules to follow – rules which many Jews still follow today.

The food that Jews are able to eat is called **kosher** (permitted) food. Food which they cannot eat is called **terefah** (forbidden) food. All meat must be slaughtered by a method known as **schechitah**: first a blessing is said over the animal and then it is killed by a single cut across the throat with a sharp knife. It is then hung upside down until all the blood has drained out of it.

In the Jewish scriptures, there is little reference to 'animal rights', but animals are seen as very valuable and they were offered as sacrifices to God in the Temple in Jerusalem.

It is clear from the scriptures that the early Jews were concerned about their animals. God gave Adam control over them:

> *Now the Lord God had formed out of the ground all the beasts of the field and all the birds of the air. He brought them to the man to see what he would name them; and whatever the man called each living creature, that was its name. So the man gave names to all the livestock, the birds of the air and all the beasts of the field.*
>
> (Genesis 2:19–20)

Knowing the name of a person or an animal was believed to give you a special spiritual power over them as it was thought that a name was part of a person.

The scriptures show that animals are to be treated with respect:

Do not muzzle an ox while it is treading out the grain.

(Deuteronomy 25:4)

A righteous man cares for the needs of his animal.

(Proverbs 12:10)

Animals are also mentioned in the Ten Commandments:

Six days you shall labour and do all your work, but the seventh day is a Sabbath to the Lord your God. On it you shall not do any work, neither you, nor your son or daughter, nor your manservant or maidservant, nor your ox, your donkey or any of your animals, nor the alien within your gates, so that your manservant and maidservant may rest, as you do.

(Deuteronomy 5:12–14)

It appears that animals were to be shown concern like human beings and to be given a day's rest.

This concern for animals in the Jewish tradition continues today. At the 1986 meeting of the World Wide Fund for Nature International held at Assisi, Rabbi Arthur Hertzberg said

…when the whole world is in peril, when the environment is in danger of being poisoned and various species, both plant and animal are becoming extinct. It is our Jewish responsibility to put the defence of the whole of nature at the very centre of our concern.

Some Jews are vegetarians through choice but there is no religious reason why they should choose this. However, some people believe that Jews should work towards becoming vegetarian and that this was God's original intention for them.

There are no clear Jewish rulings on the use of animals for scientific experiments, but many Jews believe that these experiments should be necessary and, as far as possible, suffering should be avoided.

A kosher butchers

Jews are not permitted to eat the sciatic nerve of an animal:

Therefore to this day the Israelites do not eat the tendon attached to the socket of the hip, because the socket of Jacob's hip was touched near the tendon.

(Genesis 32:32)

Or to mix dairy products and meat in the same meal:

Do not cook a young goat in its mother's milk.

(Deuteronomy 14:21)

Finally, they should not eat meat and fish together (Shulchan Arukh: Yoreh Deah 87:3).

Noah's Ark, illustration published in 1716.

Many of Judaism's teachings about animals also influenced Christianity. The early Christians were Jews and so would have followed the Jewish food laws. In the Acts of the Apostles, however, there is an account of a vision of the apostle Peter:

About noon the following day as they were on their journey and approaching the city, Peter went up on the roof to pray. He became hungry and wanted something to eat, and while the meal was being prepared, he fell into a trance. He saw heaven opened and something like a large sheet being let down to earth by its four corners. It contained all kinds of four-footed animals, as well as reptiles of the earth and birds of the air. Then a voice told him, 'Get up, Peter. Kill and eat.' 'Surely not, Lord!' Peter replied. 'I have never eaten anything impure or unclean.' The voice spoke to him a second time, 'Do not call anything impure that God has made clean.' This happened three times, and immediately the sheet was taken back to heaven.

(Acts 10:9–16)

The Lamb of God

Because of this vision, Christians were freed to eat whatever foods they wanted and, in particular, were no longer bound by the laws concerning pork and mixing meat and milk. This also meant that Christians were not required to slaughter their meat in any particular way, unlike Jews and Muslims.

Although Christians believe that they are free to eat all kinds food, in the past the Christian Church has placed some restrictions on food. Traditionally, many Christians have not eaten meat on Fridays – instead, they eat fish. This is because Friday was the day on which Jesus was crucified (Good Friday) and it was felt that meat eating was a pleasure which should be avoided on this day.

In the same way, traditionally Christians have avoided eating meat during the forty days of **Lent** which lead up to Easter. These forty days are a period of penitence and preparation for the festival of Easter – the most important festival of the Christian calendar. Lent also recalls the period when Jesus was in the desert and was tempted by the devil:

Jesus…was led by the Spirit in the desert, where for forty days he was tempted by the devil. He ate nothing during those days, and at the end of them he was hungry. The devil said to him, 'If you are the Son of God, tell this stone to become bread.' Jesus answered, 'It is written: "Man does not live on bread alone." '

(Luke 4:1–4)

In the past, Christians would hold a party before Lent to dispose of all meat. The word **carnival** comes from the Latin words *carnem levare* which mean 'to take away meat'. The idea of a carnival to mark the beginning of Lent grew up in Europe and has since spread to much of the world.

The Carnival in Venice

Although some Christians still try to 'give something up for Lent', today it is often something which they find particularly enjoyable such as chocolate, cigarettes or alcohol. There are no 'rules' about what they should do, however.

Many Christians are vegetarians but this is a matter of personal choice and there is no religious reason why they should not eat meat – Jesus himself is seen eating fish in the Bible. After the resurrection, for example, Jesus:

… showed them his hands and feet. And while they still did not believe it because of joy and amazement, he asked them, 'Do you have anything here to eat?' They gave him a piece of broiled fish, and he took it and ate it in their presence.

(Luke 24:40–43)

Also, as a Jew, Jesus would have eaten meat at the festival of Pesach (Passover).

Christians try to respect all forms of life. It is a common mistake to believe that Jesus said that 'all life is sacred', although he did respect all life. For centuries there have been discussions about whether animals have souls. However Jesus did say:

Behold the fowls of the air: for they sow not, neither do they reap, nor gather into barns; yet your heavenly Father feedeth them.

(Matthew 6:26)

His teachings suggest that birds (and animals) are valuable to God and so should be valuable to humans.

The Christian Churches have spoken out against the misuse and abuse of animals, although they have not said that necessary experiments for the preservation of human life should be stopped.

The Church of England:

> developments in science, medicine and technology should be monitored 'in the light of Christian ethical principles'.

The Methodist Church:

> The universe as a whole is a product of God's creative and imaginative will. Men and women are to be stewards and curators not exploiters of its resources, material, animal and spiritual.

The Religious Society of Friends (Quakers):

> …believe that the air, sea, earth, forests, animals and ourselves are all intimately connected, and the way in which we treat all of those things reflects on ourselves and consequently on God.

The Qur'an states that all life, animal and human, belongs to Allah:

He has created man from a sperm-drop; and behold this same (man) becomes an open disputer! And cattle He has created for you (men): from them ye derive warmth, and numerous benefits, and of their (meat) ye eat. And ye have a sense of pride and beauty in them as ye drive them home in the evening, and as ye lead them forth to pasture in the morning. And they carry your heavy loads to lands that ye could not (otherwise) reach except with souls distressed.

(Surah 16:4-7)

There is not an animal (that lives) on the earth nor a being that flies on its wings, but (forms part of) communities like you. Nothing have we omitted from the Book.

(Surah 6:38)

Humans have a duty towards all living beings. The Qur'an gives Muslims guidance about what they should and should not eat. These rules are similar to those of the Jewish tradition.

O ye people! Eat of what is on earth, lawful and good.

(Surah 2:168)

Forbidden to you (for food) are: dead meat, blood, the flesh of swine, and that on which hath been invoked the name of other than God; that which hath been killed by strangling, or by a violent blow, or by a headlong fall, or by being gored to death; that which hath been (partly) eaten by a wild animal; unless ye are able to slaughter it (in due form); that which has been sacrificed on stone (altars).

(Surah 5:4)

The restrictions cover pork, carrion (dead flesh), and any animal which has not been slaughtered by **al-dabh**, that is, according to Islamic law. A prayer, **Tasmiyyah**, is said, 'by the name of Allah', and the animal is killed by a single cutting of the throat with a sharp knife. Meat which is prepared in this way is **halal** (permitted or lawful). All food which is not halal is **haram** (forbidden).

Muslims may only hunt and kill animals and birds for the purpose of food, they are not allowed to hunt or shoot for sport. When Muslims hunt, it is not always possible for them to slaughter an animal according to al-dabh. However, if an animal or a bird is still alive when it is retrieved, it must be slain properly.

Animals which are used for hunting should be trained not to kill for themselves. The Prophet Muhammad said:

If you despatch the dog and he eats from the animal that is caught, then do not eat from the animal for he has caught it only for himself. If you despatch a dog and he kills an animal and does not eat of it, then you can eat, for the dog has caught it only for its owner.

Women preparing a goat for the festival of Id-ul-Adha, Central Africa.

The Qur'an makes reference to meat which has been killed by Jews or Christians:

> The food of the people of the Book is lawful unto you and yours is lawful unto them.
>
> (Surah 5:6)

However, this only applies to food which has been killed according to the Jewish practice of **schechitah** and over which a blessing has been said.

Muslims can eat all sea creatures provided that they live in the sea only. They are not required to kill them in any particular way. Creatures which live on land and in water, such as frogs, are forbidden.

Some Muslims may choose to be vegetarians, but there is no religious reason for them to do so. Meat plays an important part in Muslim worship. At the feast of Id–ul–Adha after the Hajj, for example, animals are slaughtered and the meat distributed to the community.

Islam is not opposed to necessary animal experimentation when it safeguards humans, but it does stress the importance of animals as part of Allah's Creation:

> *Seest thou not that it is God whose praises all beings in the heavens and on earth do celebrate, and the birds (of the air) with wings outspread?*
>
> (Surah 24:41)

There are several examples of the Prophet Muhammad's respect for all living things. During his travels, he saw an army of ants heading towards a fire, so he ordered the fire to be put out before the ants were harmed. When Muhammad was fleeing from Makkah to al–Madinah, he hid from his pursuers in a cave. A spider spun a web across the entrance and a dove nested on a ledge outside in order to protect him.

At the World Wide Fund for Nature in 1986, the Muslim representative, Dr Abdullah Omar Nasseef, stressed that humans had a responsibility to look after the earth and the animals:

> *God created mankind – a very special creation because mankind alone was created with reason and the power to think and even the means to turn against his Creator… mankind's role on earth is that of a khalifa, a viceregent or trustee of God. We are God's stewards and agents on Earth. We are not masters of this Earth; it does not belong to us to do what we wish. It belongs to God and He has entrusted us with its safekeeping …*
> *His trustees are responsible for maintaining the unity of His creation, the integrity of the Earth, its flora and fauna, its wildlife and natural environment.*

Summary

The poet Tennyson described nature as 'red in tooth and claw', yet in this country in particular, we often see animals as 'poor and helpless' and seem to have an unrealistic attitude towards them. Most people would agree that we should not treat animals cruelly and are shocked by the pictures of suffering animals released by the RSPCA, but animals have been used very successfully in many types of medical research considered too dangerous to carry out on human beings. More than 200 million animals a year are used in such experiments.

Although each of these religions believes that animals should be treated well we might ask whether they are really doing enough to protect them.

The Garden of Eden, *Breughel, Jan the elder (1568–1525).*

1 What do you understand by:

kosher and terefah

halal and haram

schechitah and al-dabh

sciatic nerve

vegetarianism and veganism

trustee or steward?

2 Explain whether you think that special rules about what people can and cannot eat are an advantage or a disadvantage for religious followers today.

3 Take one of these religions and find out how it responds to the use of animals for medical research and for cosmetic or cigarette research.

4 Explain how far religious followers should be prepared to go in the positive action which they take towards protecting 'animal rights' and why they might do this.

5 Look at some of the publicity material produced by organisations such as the RSPCA and the Anti-Vivisection League. How far do you think that people in Britain can really call themselves 'religious', or be described as a nation of animal lovers?

6 How might religious people decide between giving money to animal charities and to organisations working for children and how might they reach their decision?

7 Explain how religious followers might do more about animal welfare to fulfil their responsibilities as 'stewards of the earth.'

14 Planet earth

The phrase 'Planet earth' was first used by the poet Milton in 1667 in his poem *Paradise Lost*. In the 20th century it has become popular with science fiction writers, particularly when they want to show the earth as just one part of the universe:

...an ordinary Monday morning on the ordinary planet Earth.

Ray Bradbury

Humanity tends to behave as though the world is its property and, until very recently, people have behaved as though they can do exactly what they like with it.

A statement from the environmental agency Greenpeace puts humanity's role in the history of Planet earth into perspective:

Planet earth is 4600 million years old. We cannot imagine this length of time, but we can liken the earth to a person of 46 years of age... Dinosaurs and the great reptiles did not appear until one year ago when the planet was 45. Mammals arrived only 8 months ago: in the middle of last week, human-like apes evolved into ape-like humans, and at the weekend the last ice age covered the earth. Modern humans have been around for four hours. During the last hour, we discovered agriculture. The Industrial Revolution began about a minute ago. During those 60 seconds of time, humans have made a rubbish tip out of this beautiful world... we are really on the brink of destroying ourselves and all life on the planet.

It sometimes seems that whatever we do will cause damage to the rest of the earth.

We cannot be in any doubt that there is a problem. Every year, despite attempts at recycling, households in the United Kingdom throw away 21 million tonnes of waste. Although this seems an enormous amount, it is only three per cent of the 700 million tonnes of waste we produce every year.

It is very easy to say that you are worried about the ozone layer and traffic exhaust fumes but how many people would give up their cars? How many would walk more or use public transport in order to cut down on damage caused by traffic? Environmentalists argue that unless we do something soon the damage to the planet will be too severe to repair.

Followers of religions know the importance of safeguarding the environment. Most religions would argue that we are only on the earth as stewards and that it is our responsibility to care for it for future generations, not to destroy it. However, many also understand the need to balance this with the immediate needs of the world's population – many of whom are desperately short of food and the basic requirements for living.

This table shows how people in England and Wales were 'very worried' by environmental issues:

	1989 %	1993 %
Chemicals in rivers/seas	64	63
Toxic waste: disposal/import		63
Radioactive waste	58	60
Sewage on beaches/bathing water	59	56
Oil spills at sea/on beaches	53	52
Tropical forest destruction	44	45
Loss of plants/animals in UK		43
Ozone layer depletion	56	41
Traffic exhaust fumes/urban smog	33	40
Drinking water quality	41	38
Loss of plants/animals abroad		38
Use of insecticides/fertilisers	46	36
Loss of trees/hedgerows	34	36
Losing Green Belt land	27	35
Fumes and smoke from factories	34	35
Traffic congestion		35
Global warming	44	35
Acid rain	40	31
Litter/rubbish	33	29
Fouling by dogs	29	29
Using up United Kingdom's natural resources		27
Decay of inner cities	22	26
Household waste disposal		22
Need for more energy conservation		21
Vacant/derelict land/buildings	16	19
Not enough recycling		19
Noise	13	16

Date palms, Israel

Building a sukkah with branches and leaves.

A concern for the whole of the living world is at the centre of Jewish belief. The Tenakh (Jewish scriptures) begins with God's creation of the world:

In the beginning God created the heavens and the earth. Now the earth was formless and empty, darkness was over the surface of the deep, and the Spirit of God was hovering over the waters. And God said, 'Let there be light,' and there was light. God saw that the light was good, and he separated the light from the darkness. God called the light 'day', and the darkness he called 'night'. And there was evening, and there was morning – the first day.

(Genesis 1:1-5)

Many people no longer believe that this story should be taken literally. Even if it has to be re-thought in the light of scientific discoveries, however, it does contain teachings about the role of God in the world.
   After the creation of the world, God placed humans in charge of it:

Then God said, 'Let us make man in our image, in our likeness, and let them rule over the fish of the sea and the birds of the air, over the livestock, over all the earth, and over all the creatures that move along the ground.'

(Genesis 1:26)

It is here that humanity's stewardship of the planet begins. This stewardship of the world is seen both as a gift and an obligation.

Celebration of Creation in festivals

Every year, at the New Year festival of **Rosh Hashanah**, Jews give thanks to God for the creation of the world. Although humanity has the role of steward, the Tenakh shows that the earth is still God's possession:

The earth is the Lord's, and everything in it,
the world, and all who live in it.

(Psalm 24:1)

The scriptures also lay down regulations about how the earth is to be treated:

When you lay siege to a city for a long time, fighting against it to capture it, do not destroy its trees by putting an axe to them, because you can eat their fruit. Do not cut them down. Are the trees of the field people, that you should besiege them?

(Deuteronomy 20:19)

This respect for trees is reflected in the annual festival of
Tu B' Shevat – New Year for Trees – which takes place on the fifteenth day of the Jewish month of Shevat. This has been especially

important since the founding of the State of Israel in 1948 as Israelis have worked to reclaim the desert by a regular planting of trees. Jews around the world collect money to send to Israel for this festival.

Another regulation found in the scriptures applies to the use of the land. It was recognised that agricultural land needed to be rested if it was to continue to produce good crops. The book of Leviticus requires that once every fifty years the land should be rested in a Year of Jubilee:

Count off seven sabbaths of years – seven times seven years – so that the seven sabbaths of years amount to a period of forty-nine years. Then have the trumpet sounded everywhere on the tenth day of the seventh month; on the Day of Atonement sound the trumpet throughout your land. Consecrate the fiftieth year and proclaim liberty throughout the land to all its inhabitants. It shall be a jubilee for you; each one of you is to return to his family property and each to his own clan. The fiftieth year shall be a jubilee for you; do not sow and do not reap what grows of itself or harvest the untended vines.

(Leviticus 25:8–11)

Judaism has three harvest festivals, each linked with a particular crop:
Pesach, 15 Nisan, barley
Shavuot, 6 Sivan, wheat
Sukkot, 15 Tishri, grain and fruit

These are also known as the Pilgrim Festivals. Before the destruction of the Temple in 70CE, Jews made pilgrimages to Jerusalem for each festival in order to make offerings of the harvest to God.

At **Sukkot** Jews build a hut or booth, called a sukkah, in their gardens. This is made of branches and leaves and is decorated with fruit and vegetables. Meals are eaten inside the sukkah and Jews thank God for the harvest and for everything which he has created. The sukkah recalls the temporary huts in the Sinai desert in which the Jews lived after fleeing from Egypt.

In the Jewish prayer book there are **berachots** or blessings. Many of these are concerned with the natural world and show how Jews see the work of God in everything around them:

Blessed are You, Hashem, our God, King of the universe,
(on hearing thunder)
for His strength and His power fill the universe
(on seeing the ocean)
Who made the great sea
(on seeing very beautiful people, trees or fields)
Who has such in His universe
(on smelling a fragrance)
Who creates species of fragrance
(on smelling fruit or nuts)
Who places a good aroma into fruits

The Jewish statement made at the Conference at Assisi states the relationship between humanity and the world:

The encounter of God and man in nature is thus conceived in Judaism as a seamless web with man as the leader and custodian of the natural world. Even in the many centuries when Jews were most involved in their own immediate dangers and destiny, this universalist concern has never withered. In this century, Jews have experienced the greatest tragedy of their history when one third of their people were murdered by unnatural men and, therefore, we are today particularly sensitive to the need for a world in which each of God's creations is what He intended it to be.

Now, when the whole world is in peril, when the environment is in danger of being poisoned and various species, both plant and animal, are becoming extinct, it is our Jewish responsibility to put the defence of the whole of nature at the very centre of our concern. Two men were out on the water in a rowboat. Suddenly, one of them started to saw under his feet. He maintained that it was his right to do whatever he wished with the place which belonged to him. The other answered him that they were in the rowboat together; the hole that he was making would sink both of them.

(Vayikra Rabbah 4:6)

Christian attitudes towards the environment are based largely on the Old Testament. God's role as Creator of the universe and everything in it is emphasised in the statement of belief called the Nicene Creed:

We believe in one God, the Father, the almighty,
maker of heaven and earth,
of all that is,
seen and unseen.

We believe in one Lord, Jesus Christ,
the only Son of God,
eternally begotten of the Father,
God from God, Light from Light,
true God from true God,
begotten, not made,
of one Being with the Father.
Through him all things were made.

In the New Testament, Jesus also talks about God's Creation when he is showing how important humans are:

Consider how the lilies grow. They do not labour or spin. Yet I tell you, not even Solomon in all his splendour was dressed like one of these. If that is how God clothes the grass of the field, which is here today, and tomorrow is thrown into the fire, how much more will he clothe you, O you of little faith!
(Luke 12:27–28)

Celebration of Creation in festivals

Harvest Festival, a celebration which takes place in many Churches in the autumn, is also an opportunity for Christians to thank God for continuing to feed them and provide for them. Churches and many schools collect together produce which has been grown locally, if possible. After thanking God for the harvest, the produce is usually distributed to poor people or the elderly.

The festival of Easter celebrates Jesus' resurrection from death after he was executed on the cross. It is also seen as the beginning of spring and as a celebration of new life and this is represented in a mostly secular way by the giving of eggs and spring flowers.

A Harvest Festival prayer

Almighty and everlasting God, we offer you our hearty thanks for your fatherly goodness and care in giving us the fruits of the earth in their seasons.
Give us grace to use them rightly,
to your glory,
for our own well-being,
and for the relief of those in need.

Easter food

In recent years the Christian Churches have become very concerned with environmental issues. In 1988, Pope John Paul II issued an Encyclical called *Sollicitudo Rei Socialis* (On Social Concerns) in which he said:

The earth and all life on it is a gift from God given us to share and develop, not to dominate and exploit.
Our actions have consequences for the rights of others and for the resources of the earth.
The goods of the earth and the beauties of nature are to be enjoyed and celebrated as well as consumed.
We have the responsibility to create a balanced policy between consumption and conservation.
We must consider the welfare of future generations in our planning for and utilisation of the earth's resources.

These verses are from a poem by Kate Compston, a Christian minister:

Great Spirit,
still brooding over the world —

We hear the cry of the earth,
we see the sorrow of the land
raped and plundered in our greed
for its varied resources.

We hear the cry of the waters,
we see the sorrow of stream and ocean
polluted by the poisons
we release into them…

Please teach us
a proper sensitivity
towards your feeling creation
a proper simplicity
in the way we live in our environment
a proper appreciation
of the connectedness of all things
a proper respect
for the shalom of the universe.

We turn from our arrogant ways
to seek you again, Lord of all life,
Redeem us and redeem your world
and heal its wounds and dry its tears.
May our response to you bear fruit
in a fresh sense of responsibility
towards everything you have created.

St Francis of Assisi was born in 1181 and died in 1226. He was particularly concerned with God's creation and wrote a prayer known as the *Canticle of the Sun*:

O Most High, Almighty, good Lord God, to you belong praise, glory, honour, and all blessing!
Praised be my Lord God for all his creatures, especially for our brother the sun who brings us the day and who brings us the light; far is he and shines with a very great splendour;
O Lord, he signifies you to us.
Praised be my Lord for our sister the moon, and for the stars, which he has set clear and lovely in heaven.
Praised be my Lord for our brother the wind, and for the air and clouds, calms and all weather by which you uphold life in all creatures.

The Cornfield, *John Constable (1776–1837)*

115

According to Islam teaching, Allah is the Creator of the world and humans are only here as vice-regents or trustees. Their task is not to destroy the world but to safeguard it for God and for future generations.

So set thou thy face steadily and truly to the Faith: (establish) God's handiwork according to the pattern on which He has made mankind: no change (let there be) in the work (wrought) by God.

(Surah 30:30)

God is He who raised the heavens without any pillars that ye can see; is firmly established on the Throne (of Authority); He has subjected the sun and the moons (to his Law)! Each one runs (its course) for a term appointed. He doth regulate all affairs, explaining the signs in detail, that ye may believe with certainty in the meeting with your Lord. And it is He who spread out the earth, and set thereon mountains standing firm, and (flowing) rivers: and fruit of every kind He made in pairs, two and two: He draweth the night as a veil over the day. Behold, verily in these things there are signs for those who consider!

(Surah 13:2-3)

There is no 'harvest festival' in Islam but this does not mean that Muslims are not constantly giving thanks to Allah for his Creation and for their food.

The Earth is green and beautiful, and Allah has appointed you his stewards over it.
The whole earth has been created a place of worship, pure and clean.
Whoever plants a tree and diligently looks after it until it matures and bears fruit is rewarded.
If a Muslim plants a tree or sows a field and humans and beasts and birds eat from it, all of it is love on his part.

(Hadith)

Both Judaism and Christianity have calendars which are based on the regular cycle of seasons through spring, summer, autumn and winter. Many of the festivals of these two religions are tied in to seasonal changes and began in the customs and celebrations of earlier religions. Islam, however, has a religious year which, at 354 days, is shorter than the Western calendar year of approximately 365 days. The calendar is based on a 30 year cycle of 360 lunar months which vary between 29 and 30 days. By doing this, Islam avoids any link to earlier pagan feasts and so the Muslim religious festivals fall at a different time from year to year.

Islam has always been known for its scientific knowledge and discoveries. Muslim medicine traditionally concentrated on the use of drugs and herbs rather than on surgery. Ibn Sina, who died in 1037 CE described how epidemics spread and al-Razi (d. 925 CE) was the first scientist to distinguish between smallpox and measles. Remembering also that many traditional Muslim countries are dry and arid with large areas of desert, it is not surprising that Islam has shown itself particularly concerned with plant life and the environment.

At the World Wide Fund for Nature at Assisi in 1986, the Muslim representative, Dr Abdullah Omar Nasseef, stressed the human responsibility to look after the earth:

The central concept of Islam is tawheed or the Unity of God. Allah is Unity; and His Unity is also reflected in the unity of mankind, and the unity of man and nature. His trustees are responsible for maintaining the unity of His creation, the integrity of the Earth, its flora and fauna, its wildlife and natural environment. Unity cannot be had by discord, by setting one need against another or letting one end predominate over another; it is maintained by balance and harmony. There Muslims say that Islam is the middle path and we will be answerable for how we have walked this path, how we have maintained balance and harmony in the whole of creation around us.

So unity, trusteeship and accountability, that is tawheed, khalifa and akhrah, the three central concepts of Islam, are also the pillars of the environmental ethics of Islam. They constitute the basic values taught by the Qur'an. It is these values which led Muhammad, the Prophet of Islam, to say: 'Whoever plants a tree and diligently looks after it until it matures and bears fruit is rewarded'.

Islam sees that humans are responsible for looking after the world which God created and for the well-being of all humanity.

Summary

Followers of the world's religions believe that God created the world for them to live in. They believe that they have a duty to safeguard that world for future generations of all faiths and that they must take an active part in ensuring that greed and ignorance do not destroy the world.

Creation Harvest Liturgy
Brothers and sisters in creation, we covenant this day with you and with all creation yet to be;
With every living Creature and all that contains and sustains you.
With all that is on earth and with the earth itself,
With all that lives in the water and with the waters themselves;
With all that flies in the skies and with the sky itself. We establish this covenant, that all our powers will be used to prevent your destruction. We confess that it is our own kind who put you at risk of death. We ask you for your trust and as a symbol of our intention we mark our covenant with you by the rainbow.
This is the sign of the covenant between ourselves and every living thing that is found on the earth.

1 What do you understand by:

the environment

Planet earth

nature

recycling

developing countries

vice-regent?

2 Explain why many religions feel that humanity has been given responsibility for the earth.

3 Take one of these religions and find out what positive steps it is taking towards safeguarding the environment and why it feels that it should be doing this.

4 Explain how far religious followers should be prepared to go in the positive action towards the environment.

5 Read the table at the beginning of this chapter. What do you think are the most important areas to be concerned about?

6 Look at some of the materials produced by groups such as Greenpeace and consider whether they are saying the right things to people about the environment. Could you produce something about an area which you are particularly concerned about which you think would be more effective?

7 Explain how religious people might make decisions about whether they should concentrate their energies on 'feeding the world' or 'safeguarding the environment'.

8 In your opinion, should people be prepared to give up the 'luxuries of life' in order to ensure the planet for future generations.

Glossary

Aron Hakodesh (Judaism) Holy Ark. The focal point of the synagogue, containing Torah scrolls.

Adhan (Islam) call to prayer

Agnostic Someone who believes that you cannot know whether there is a God or not.

Al-dabh (Islam) Method of slaughtering animals for food.

Al-Fatihah (Islam) The Opener. Surah 1 of the Qur'an. Recited at least 17 times daily during the five times of salah.

Al-Mi'raj (Islam) The ascent through the heavens of the Prophet Muhammad,

Al-Qadr (Islam) A belief that Allah has laid down a pre-determined course for the world and knows the destiny of every living creature.

Akhirah (Islam) Everlasting life after death - the hereafter.

Amish (Christian) A strict sect of the Mennonite church in the United States. Followers still live as their predecessors did in the 17th century.

Anarchic Without rule or government, lawless.

Atheist Someone who believes that God does not exist.

Atonement (Christian) Reconciliation between God and humanity; restoring a relationship broken by sin.

Beth Din (Judaism) Jewish Court

Bimah (Judaism) Dais. Raised platform primarily for reading the Torah in the synagogue.

Buddhism The religious system founded by the Buddha, Siddatha Gotama.

Celibate Unmarried, single; someone who has vowed or promised not to marry.

Charismatic (Christianity) A modern movement within the Church, emphasising spiritual gifts, such as healing or speaking with tongues.

Chazan (Judaism) Leader of reading, singing and chanting in the Cantor services of some synagogues.

Conscience Inward knowledge, consciousness; innermost thought, mind.

Cosmological argument The universe was created by a 'first cause' which was God.

Creed (Christianity) Summary statement of religious beliefs, often recited in worship, especially the Apostles' and Nicene Creeds.

Eucharist (Christianity) Thanksgiving. A service celebrating the sacrificial death and resurrection of Jesus Christ, using elements of bread and wine.

Free will Having the choice of what to do without being controlled in any way.

Gemilut Hasadim (Judaism) A form of charity. Literally it means 'kind actions' and covers all sorts of charitable work.

Glossolalia (Christianity) Speaking in tongues under the influence of the Holy Spirit.

Gnosticism The religion of the Gnostics. A group who were probably in existence at the same time as Christianity came into being.

Halakhah (Judaism) The Way. The code of conduct encompassing all aspects of Jewish life. Going with God.

Hadith (Islam) Saying; report; account. The sayings of the Prophet Muhammad.

Hajj (Islam) Annual pilgrimage to Makkah, which each Muslim must undertake at least once in a lifetime if he or she has the health and wealth.

Halal (Islam) Any action or thing which is permitted or lawful.

Haram (Islam) Anything unlawful or not permitted.

Hinduism The religion of the Hindus, a development of the ancient Brahmanism with many later additions.

Holocaust The mass murder of the Jews, and others, by the Nazis in the war of 1939-1945.

Huppah (Judaism) Canopy used for a wedding ceremony, under which the bride and groom stand.

Hutterites Members of an Anabaptist sect established by Jacob Hutter in Moravia, or of immigrant communities in North America having similar beliefs.

Imam (Islam) Leader. A person who leads the communal prayer, or a founder of an Islamic school of jurisprudence.

Iman (Islam) Faith

Jain A member of a non-Brahminical East Indian sect, established about the sixth century BCE, the principal doctrines of which closely resemble those of Buddhism. Jihad (Islam).

Ketubah (Judaism) Document that defines rights and obligations within Jewish marriage.

Khalifah (Islam) Successor; inheritor; custodian; vice-regent or trustee of God.

Kosher (Judaism) Fit; proper. Foods permitted by Jewish dietary laws.

Lent (Christianity) Penitential season. The 40 days leading up to Easter.

Mahr (Islam) Marriage dowry.

Masjid (Islam) Place of prostration. Mosque.

Meditation Continuous thought or musing upon one subject or series of subjects for a religious purpose.

Menorah (Judaism) Seven-branched candelabrum which was lit daily in the Temple.

Mikveh (Judaism) Ritual bath used for the immersion of people and objects.

Miracle A marvellous event, which cannot have been brought about by human power or by the operation of any natural agency, and is therefore thought to be an act of God.

Mitzvot (Judaism) Commandment. The Torah contains 613 mitzvot. Commonly used to describe good deeds.

Moonies A nickname for a member of the Unification Church.

Niddah (Judaism) Laws of family purity.

Numinous The presence of god which inspires awe and reverence.

Ontological argument Describing God as 'that than which nothing greater can be conceived'.

Paganism The religious belief and practices of pagans.

Parousia (Christianity) Presence. The Second Coming or return of Jesus Christ.

Polygamy The practice or custom according to which one man has several wives.

Polyandry The practice or custom according to which one woman has two or more husbands at the same time.

Purgatory (Christianity) An intermediate place between heaven and hell.

Pushke (Judaism) A collection box for charity.

Qur'an (Islam) That which is read or recited. The Divine Book revealed to the Prophet Muhammad, Allah's final revelation to humankind.

Rastafarianism A black religious movement from Jamaica which worships Haile Selassie of Ethopia.

Resurrection (Christianity) (i) The rising from the dead of Jesus Christ on the third day after the crucifixion . (ii) The rising from the dead of believers at the Last Day. (iii) The new, or risen, life of Christians.

Revelation Knowledge given to human beings by God.

Salah (Islam) Prescribed communication with, and worship of, Allah, performed under specific conditions, in the manner taught by the Prophet Muhammad and recited in the Arabic language. The five daily times of salah are fixed by Allah.

Sawm (Islam) Fasting from just before dawn until sunset. Abstinence is required, from all food and drink (including water) as well as smoking and conjugal relations.

Schechitah (Judaism) Jewish method of slaughtering meat.

Scientology A system of beliefs based on the study of knowledge and claiming to develop the highest abilities of its members, founded in 1951 by L. Ron Hubbard.

Shahadah (Islam) Declaration of faith, which consists of the statement, 'There is no god except Allah, Muhammad is the Messenger of Allah'.

Shari'ah (Islam) Islamic law based upon the Qur'an and Sunnah

Shema (Judaism) Major Jewish prayer affirming belief in one God. The Shema is found in the Torah.

Shoah (Judaism) Desolation. The suffering experienced by European Jews at the hands of the Nazis, including the systematic murder of six million Jews between 1933 and 1945.

Sikhism Religion which follows of the teachings of Guru Nanak Dev Ji and the later Gurus.

Sukkot (Judaism) One of three biblical pilgrim festivals, Sukkot is celebrated in the autumn.

Sunnah (Islam) Model practices, customs and traditions of the Prophet Muhammad.

Surah (Islam) Division of the Qur'an (114 in all).

Tallit (Judaism) Prayer shawl. Four-cornered garment with fringes.

Talmud (Judaism) The Oral Torah. Mishnah and Gemara, collected together.

Tawhid (Islam) Belief in the Oneness of Allah – absolute monotheism.

Teleological argument The argument from design.

Tenakh (Judaism) The collected 24 books of the Jewish Bible, comprising three sections: Torah, Nevi'im, and Ketuvim (Te;Na;Kh).

Terefah (Judaism) forbidden

Torah (Judaism) Law; teaching. The Five Books of Moses.

Trinity (Christianity) Three persons in one God; doctrine of the threefold nature of God-Father, Son and Holy Spirit.

zakah (Islam) Purification of wealth by payment of annual welfare due.

Zoroastrianism One of the oldest religions in the world taught by Zoroaster and his followers.

Short Course syllabus overview

	EdExcel A	MEG B	NEAB B	SEG	WJEC
What is God?	✓	✓	✓	✓	✓
How can we 'know'?					
The case of Science v. Religion	✓	✓	✓	✓	✓
Good or bad?	✓	✓	✓	✓	✓
Prayer, worship and the 'Holy Other'	✓	✓	✓	✓	✓
But it's not fair	✓	✓	✓	✓	✓
Is anything really sacred?	✓	✓	✓	✓	✓
A question of dying	✓	✓	✓	✓	✓
Are love and sex the same thing?	✓	✓	✓	✓	✓
Till death (or something else) us do part	✓	✓	✓	✓	✓
I'm all right Jack (or Jill)	✓	✓	✓	✓	✓
Soap box or soap opera?	✓				
A four-legged friend	✓	✓	✓	✓	✓
Planet earth	✓	✓	✓	✓	✓

Exam-type questions

1 **What is 'God'?**
(a) How do people know that God exists?
(b) What do religious people mean when they say that God loves them?
(c) 'If people could see God everyone would be religious.'
Do you agree? Give reasons to support your answer and show that you have thought about different points of view.

2 **How can we 'know'?**
(a) What do people mean when they use the word 'revelation'?
(b) Explain how and why people may treat their holy books with great respect.
(d) 'A holy book is just like any other book; it is not anything special.'
Do you agree? Give reasons to support your answer and show that you have thought about different points of view.

3 **The case of Science *v.* Religion**
(a) Give a brief explanation of what people mean when they talk about 'Creation' and 'evolution'.
(b) Explain why some religious people may find it difficult to accept the account of Creation in their holy books while others do not.
(c) 'Stories about Creation are just fairy tales.'
Do you agree? Give reasons to support your answer and show that you have thought about different points of view.

4 **Good or bad?**
(a) Explain what religious people believe about the power of evil and its effect on human beings.
(b) Explain how religious people should respond when they see people suffering.
(c) 'If God really cared he would not let us suffer.'
Do you agree? Give reasons to support your answer and show that you have thought about different points of view.

5 **Prayer, worship and the 'Holy Other'**
(a) Describe some of the ways in which people might worship at home and in public.
(b) People often say that they have been guided by God. Explain the ways in which this guidance might be received.
(c) 'Worship is the most important part of a person's life.'
Do you agree? Give reasons to support your answer and show that you have thought about different points of view.

6 **But it's not fair**

(a) Explain the religious teaching about war and peace.

(b) Explain why religious people might sometimes feel that it is necessary to fight.

(c) 'All religious people must be pacifists.'

Do you agree? Give reasons to support your answer and show that you have thought about different points of view.

7 **Is anything really sacred?**

(a) What are the reasons for people saying that life is sacred?

(b) Explain what people believe about the value of the individual. You may refer to particular examples such as abortion and euthanasia.

(c) 'Killing people or letting them die is wrong whatever the circumstances.'

Do you agree? Give reasons to support your answer and show that you have thought about different points of view.

8 **A question of dying**

(a) What might some religious people believe will happen when they die?

(b) How might their beliefs about death affect the way in which people live their lives?

(c) 'It is wrong for religious people to mourn and be unhappy at a funeral.'

Do you agree? Give reasons to support your answer and show that you have thought about different points of view.

9 **Are love and sex the same thing?**

(a) What religious teachings might affect a person's decision to enter into a sexual relationship?

(b) Why do some religions say that homosexuality is wrong?

(c) 'People who do not live in a loving relationship must always be celibate.'

Do you agree? Give reasons to support your answer and show that you have thought about different points of view.

10 **Till death (or something else) us do part**

(a) What are the religious reasons for people to be married?

(b) Explain why some religious people might feel that it was right for them to have a divorce.

(c) 'People should try living together before they are married to avoid any problems later.'

Do you agree? Give reasons to support your answer and show that you have thought about different points of view.

11 I'm all right Jack (or Jill)

(a) What does religion teach about how people should behave towards the poor?

(b) Explain how religious people should deal with poverty in developing countries.

(c) 'There is so much poverty that it is not even worth trying to do anything about it.'
Do you agree? Give reasons to support your answer and show that you have thought about different points of view.

12 Soap box or soap opera?

(a) In what ways do different types of media deal with religious matters?

(b) Explain why some religious people might feel that the media is dangerous.

(c) 'Any publicity is good publicity, even when it is about religion.'
Do you agree? Give reasons to support your answer and show that you have thought about different points of view.

13 A four-legged friend

(a) What religious teachings are particularly important when people are talking about the way in which animals are treated?

(b) Explain how religious beliefs might affect the way in which people treat animals.

(c) 'Animals are not as important as people and therefore there is no problem about using them for research.'
Do you agree? Give reasons to support your answer and show that you have thought about different points of view.

14 Planet earth

(a) What religious teachings are particularly important when people are talking about caring for the environment?

(b) Explain how religious beliefs might affect what people eat and when.

(c) 'Religious people should be concerned about other human beings and not the environment.'
Do you agree? Give reasons to support your answer and show that you have thought about different points of view.

Index

126

Thomas Nelson and Sons Ltd
Nelson House Mayfield Road
Walton-on-Thames Surrey
KT12 5PL UK

Thomas Nelson Australia
102 Dodds Street
South Melbourne
Victoria 3205 Australia

Nelson Canada
1120 Birchmount Road
Scarborough Ontario
M1K 5G4 Canada

© Jon Mayled 1997

First published by Thomas Nelson and Sons Ltd 1997

ɪⓉⓅ® Thomas Nelson is an International Thomson Publishing Company

ɪⓉⓅ® is used under licence

ISBN 0-17-437034-2
NPN 9 8 7 6 5 4 3 2 1

Acknowledgements
The publishers are grateful to the following for permission to reproduce copyright material:
Advertising Archives p. 100 (bottom); BBC p. 96; Bridgeman pp. 9 (top right), 10, 11, 14, 34, 46, 47, 67, 78, 79, 83 (top), 110, 115; Gamma pp. 19 (left), 24, 27, 107; Hutchison Library pp. 63; Jewish Care p. 88; Panos Pictures p. 65; Range/Bettmann/AFP p. 64; Rex Features pp. 15 (top), 19 (bottom right), 21, 52, 59 (both), 98 (both), 99 (right), 100 (top); Images pp. 66, 69; Jon Mayled p. 108; David Rose p. 89, 95, 113; RSPCA p. 103; Peter Sanders p. 76, Image Select pp. 4, 9 (bottom), 17 (top), 23, 26, 28, 29, 33, 42, 44, 81, 99 (left), 105 (right), 106, 114 (top); Tony Stone pp. 12, 13 (right), 58, 74 (both), 85 (left), 91 (bottom), 94, 112, 114 (bottom), 116, 117; Trip pp. 5, 13 (bottom), 15 (bottom), 17 (bottom), 19 (top), 20, 31, 49, 56, 57, 60, 61, 68, 71 (both), 72, 73, 83 (bottom), 85 (right), 86, 87, 91 (top), 93, 105 (left);

Printed in Croatia.